McLa...

Homework Pocket Dictionary

DAMAND Promotions
Poway, California

Dan J. McLaughlin Sr

Published by
DAMAND Promotions
P.O. Box 911
Poway, CA 92074

ISBN 1-892565-85-3

Bulk Order Information

Email
Danmc10@aol.com

Website
Damand.com

Table of Contents

Language Arts

Adjectives	3
Adverbs	6
Capitalization	14
Cause & Effect	16
Comma	18
Compounds, subject, sentence	19
Conjunctions	22
Context	23
Contractions	23
Digraph	27
Footnotes	29
Homonym	30
Nouns	34
Outlining	39
Predicates	45
Prefix	46
Prepositions	47
Punctuation	49
Sentences	51
Simile	52
Subjects	53
Subject - Verb Agreement	54
Suffix	55

Topic Sentence   60
Verbs   60
Writing Process   65

Math

Addition   72
Subtraction   78
Multiplication   84
Division   90
Fractions   98
Decimals   114
Geometry   120
Algebra   129
General Math Terms   153

Language Arts

Adverbs	6
Bibliography	10
Conjunctions	22
Footnotes	29
Nouns	34
Participles	43
Prepositions	47
Sentences	51
Verbs	60

Language Arts

Abbreviations

Shortened form of a word usually beginning with a capital letter and sometimes ending with a period. Some words that can be abbreviated are: titles, words used in addresses, words used in business, states, proper names, and words that have capital letters in their title.

EXAMPLES:

TV ~ Television

PO ~ Post Office

PE ~ Physical Education

CA ~ California

Amanda L. ~ Amanda Leah

Acronym

Are words that are formed from the first letter of other words as a title.

EXAMPLES:

NATO ~ **N**orth **A**tlantic **T**reaty **O**rganization

Language Arts

Adjective

A word used to describe a noun or pronoun. Adjectives tell what kind, how many, or which one.

EXAMPLES:

**What Kind*

The *female* tiger slept all day.

Adjective: *female*

**How Many*

The *two* tigers slept all day.

Adjective: *two*

**Which One*

The *big* tiger slept all day.

Adjective: *big*

Language Arts

Adjective - demonstrative (this, that, these, those)
   A special kind of adjective used before a noun or before another adjective.   It tells which one the speaker is talking about.   The words **this** and **these** refer to nouns close to the speaker.   The words **that** and **those** are nouns farther away.

EXAMPLES:

*This   (singular - just one)

This is a great hamburger!

Demonstrative Adjective: *This*

*These   (plural - more than one)

These hamburgers are great!

Demonstrative Adjective: *These*

*That   (singular - just one)

Please pass *that* large glass.

Demonstrative Adjective: *that*

*Those   (plural - more than one)

Please pass *those* large glasses.

Demonstrative Adjective: *those*

Language Arts

Adjective - predicate
Follows a linking verb and describes or modifies the subject.

EXAMPLE:

The story is ***wonderful.***

Subject: *story*

Linking Verb: *is*

Predicate Adjective: *wonderful*

Adjective - proper
Formed from a proper noun and capitalized. It helps describe the noun.

EXAMPLES:

Those tigers are from India.

They are ***Indian*** tigers.

Proper Adjective: *Indian*

That is an ***American*** car.

Proper Adjective: *American*

Language Arts

Adverb

Word that describes a verb and sometimes end in -ly. Adverbs tell you when, how, how much, or where an action happens.

EXAMPLES:

When (later, often, next, first, etc.)

We can go to the movie *later* today.

Adverb: *later*

How (slowly, hard, fast, quietly, etc.)

The man ran *quickly* down the stairs.

Adverb: *quickly*

Where (inside, here, far, forward, etc.)

Please go *inside* and get the card game.

Adverb: *inside*

Ending in ly

Leah writes *beautifully*.

Adverb: *beautifully*

Language Arts

Affix

Can be placed at the beginning or end of the base word as either a prefix or suffix.

EXAMPLE:

Prefix: **un** ~ happy   **un**happy

Suffix: quick ~ **ly**   quick**ly**

Alliteration

The repeating of the first sound of each word.

EXAMPLE:

Mandy **m**ay **m**ake **m**ore **m**uffins on **M**onday.

Alliteration: *m*

Analogy

Compares different things that may or may not be directly related.

EXAMPLE:

The Dodgers and the Celtics are both very disciplined teams.

Analogy: The *Dodgers* are a baseball team and the *Celtics* are a basketball team but a comparison was made about each team being the same in the area of discipline.

Language Arts

Antonym
   A word and its opposite.

   EXAMPLES:

   left ~ right; up ~ down; in ~ out; fast ~ slow;
   right ~ wrong; good ~ bad; strong ~ weak

Appositive
   A word or phrase that follows a noun and gives more
   information about it. Appositives are generally set off
   by commas.

   EXAMPLE:

   Mickey Mantle, *a Yankee great*, hit 536 homeruns
   in his career.

   Appositive: *a Yankee great*

Article (a, an, the)
   A special kind of adjective used before a noun or
   before another adjective.

   EXAMPLE:

   It is time for Emilie Lynn to take *a* nap.

   Article: *a*

Language Arts

Author's Purpose

When authors write a story they are trying to provide information, entertainment, or they are attempting to persuade the reader.

EXAMPLES:

1. A *newspaper* article *informs* the reader.
2. A *mystery* story *entertains* the reader.
3. An *editorial* tries to *persuade* the reader.

Autobiography

An author's story of their own life.

EXAMPLE: Underline Autobiographies

The Diary of Anne Frank

The Autobiography of Benjamin Franklin

Base Word

A word that has a prefix or suffix added to change the meaning or tense of the original word.

Remember:

Prefix is added to the *beginning* of the word.
Suffix is added to the *end* of the word.

Language Arts

Base Word continued

EXAMPLES:

happy is the base word for *unhappy*
cycle is the base word for *bicycle*
write is the base word for *rewrite*
room is the base word for *roomy*
soft is the base word for *softly*
ship is the base word for *shipment*
teach is the base word for *teacher*

Bibliography

A list of sources that credits other people for information you use in a research paper. It is important that basic data is included for each source so that the reader can trace the information back to the original material.

EXAMPLES:

Book
List in the following order: author (name: last, first), name of book, edition, city of publisher, publisher, year of publication.
See example below:

McLaughlin, D. J. <u>The Homework Encyclopedia</u>,
    2d ed. San Diego: DAMAND
    Publishing, 2007.

Language Arts

Magazine
List in the following order: name of article, magazine, date (in parentheses), and page number. *See example below:*

"Elway Finally Gets One, Denver Wins the
Superbowl," <u>Sport Illustrated</u>.
(February 6, 1998), p. 10.

Newspaper
List in the following order: author, title of article, newspaper, date (in parentheses), page and column number. *See example below:*

Davidson, Seth "USC beats Arizona State
21-14 to Win the College World Series,"
<u>Imperial Valley Press</u>. (May 13, 1998),
p. 13, col. 2

CD-ROM Database
List in the following order: name of author, publication information for the printed source (including title and date of print publication), title of the database (underlined), publication medium (CD-ROM), name of the vendor (if relevant), electronic publication date.

Scott, George C. "How to Divide Mixed
Numbers." <u>Homework Encyclopedia</u>.
13 Jul. 12009: BL. Newsbank.
CD-ROM. Mar. 2009.

Language Arts

Internet

List in the following order: author, title of text (underlined), publication information for the printed source, publication medium (online), name of the repository of the electronic text (such as a university library, etc.), name of computer network, date of access, electronic address used to access the document preceded by the word *"Available."*

Fudd, Elmer. <u>That Wrascally Wabbit</u>. Ed.
    Fran Johnstone. Zodiac Signs. New
    York: Oxford, 1986. Online. U of
    Chapman Lib. Internet. 26 Dec. 1985.
    Available FTP: etext.chapman.edu.

Biography

True story of a person's life. Written by someone who knows, studied, or has interviewed the subject. Ideally, a biography includes birth and death, education, ambition, work, conflicts, relationships, and other interesting aspects of the person's life written as a unique book or paper.

Language Arts

Book - parts of

Appendix
The location where the table, charts and graphs, lists, or diagrams are listed. You can find the appendix in the back of the book.

Glossary
Contains definitions to words used in the book and arranged in alphabetical order. Glossaries are generally located at the end of the book and usually precede bibliographies.

Index
A listing of all the subjects, names, and concepts in the book arranged in alphabetical order with page numbers that correspond to the book.

Table of Contents
Usually follows the Title Page. It lists the chapter or units and gives the page numbers. Chapters are listed in the order they appear in the book.

Title Page
Usually the first printed page of the book telling the title, author, publishing company, and where the book was published.

Language Arts

Capitalization

The first word of every sentence must be capitalized. This tells the reader that a new sentence and a new thought has begun. Also required with an abbreviation and proper nouns are also capitalized.

EXAMPLES:

Also Capitalize:

The pronoun I and its contractions:

Michael Jordan and **I** went to the basketball game. **I'll** do my homework after school.

Titles or their abbreviations when used with a person's name:

Dr. **D**. **J**. **M**cLaughlin

Proper Adjectives:

Those are **A**merican cars.

Days: **S**aturday

Months: **A**ugust

Holidays: **M**emorial **D**ay

Language Arts

Capitalization continued

Names of buildings and companies:

White **H**ouse

Damand **P**romotions

First, last, and all important words in a title:

The **M**onster from **M**yrtle **S**treet

All words in the greeting and first word in the closing of a letter:

Dear **D**ad,

Sincerely yours,

Proper names, streets, cities, states, and countries:

Capt. **P**icard lives at 1701 **N**omad **S**treet.

Dallas is in the state of **T**exas.

Amy **F**rederickson was born in **C**alifornia.

Language Arts

Cause and Effect

Cause is why something happens and the *effect* is the result. The cause will always happen <u>first</u> and the effect will happen <u>second</u>.

EXAMPLES:

Andrea *swung the bat* and **hit a homerun**.

Cause: *swung the bat*
Effect: **hit a homerun**

John Elway threw a pass and it was caught for a **touchdown**.

Cause: *threw a pass*
Effect: **touchdown**

Everyone in our class received a 100% on the spelling test so we had a **pizza party**.

Cause: *100% on our spelling test*
Effect: **pizza party**

Characterization

When the author develops the traits and qualities of characters in a story. The author may include their honesty, eye color, hobbies, etc.

Language Arts

Classifying

Grouping items by choosing the things most important to the items being classified. Items can be grouped in a variety of ways.

EXAMPLE:

Dinosaurs can be classified by what they eat. One group can be carnivorous (meat eaters) and the other herbivores (plant eaters). We can put the dinosaurs in the proper group.

Carnivorous	**Herbivores**
Tyrannosaurus	*Triceratops*
Allosaurus	*Stegosaurus*
Velociraptor	*Brachiosaurus*
Ceratosaurus	*Apatosaurus*

We can also classify dinosaurs as two-legged, four-legged, by size, or habitat.

Clipped Words

Words that have been shortened. Clipped words are **not** abbreviations.

EXAMPLES:

mathematics ~ math
telephone ~ phone
advertisement ~ ad
airplane ~ plane

Language Arts

Comma (,)

A pause that helps to make a sentence clear.

EXAMPLES:

1. After introductory words (yes, well, no, etc.).
   Well, will you please clean your room?

2. In a series of three or more items.
   Superman, Batman, and Spiderman
   are all superheroes.

3. Separating two or more adjectives.
   A fresh, ripe apple was on the table.

4. Before the conjunction in a compound
   sentence.
   Some of the kids were playing ball,
   but other kids were eating a snack.

5. Separate nouns in a direct address.
   Tammi, Bill please help me set the table?

6. Use between a city and state.
   Poway, California

7. After a greeting in a friendly letter.
   Dear Nakita,

8. After a closing in a letter.
   Sincerely yours,

Language Arts

Compound Sentence

Two or more independent clauses (simple sentences) joined together by a <u>conjunction or a linking adverb</u>. A comma *can* be used to separate the parts of the compound sentence.

Conjunctions: *and, or, but*
Linking Adverbs: *however, therefore, also, thus*

EXAMPLE: *and*

There are five hundred fish in the pond.
There are twenty goldfish in the pond.

Compound Sentence:
There are five hundred fish in the pond *and* twenty of them are goldfish.

EXAMPLE: *or*

Compound Sentence: Do you want to go to the movies *or* do you want to go shopping?

EXAMPLE: *but*

Compound Sentence:
There are five hundred fish in the pond *but* only twenty are sharks.

EXAMPLE: *however, also, therefore, thus*

Antz was a good movie, ***however***, more people went to see *Godzilla*.

Language Arts

Compound Subject

When two or more simple subjects are combined using a conjunction (or/and). Combine the two simple subjects in the following sentence.

EXAMPLE:

Dan will go to school. Glenda will go to school.

Compound Sentence:

Dan *and* Glenda will go to school.

Compound Subjects: Dan *and* Glenda

Compound Word

Two words joined together to make one word.

Such as:

volleyball = volley + ball

baseball = base + ball

classroom = class + room

chalkboard = chalk + board

freetime = free + time

basketball = basket + ball

Language Arts

Concept Mapping

This is one way to organize ideas and information. This may include outlining, story mapping, or a story web. Once ideas are organized then it is a simple matter of composing these ideas in a creative and logical sequence. Sentences should use descriptive words and terms to give the reader a mental picture.

Settings	**Title**	*Characters*
Simulator Room	**Star Trek II**	Saavik
		Spock
		McCoy
		Kirk
		Sulu
		Uhura

List a setting and all the characters in that setting. Describe the setting and character using colorful words (adjectives & adverbs).

Title: Star Trek II, The Wrath of Khan

Opening scene: In a simulator room depicting the bridge of the Enterprise.

Characters: Spock, McCoy, Kirk, Saavik

How many sentences can we write just with this scene alone?

Language Arts

Conflict

A problem that may pit a character against a force of nature or against another character. It may also concern a character and his or her emotions. Most movies and books have conflict.

EXAMPLE: *Conflict ~ against one another*

Batman and the Riddler were in conflict.

Conjunction

Conjunctions connect words or groups of words. Conjunctions join the parts of compound subjects, compound predicates, and compound sentences.

EXAMPLE:

Fifty students are in the class **and** twenty students are girls.

Conjunction: *and*

Common Conjunctions:

both...and; either...or; neither...nor

Language Arts

Context

It is a way you can tell the meaning of a word or term by examining the other words in the sentence. This is helpful when we don't know the meaning of the word in a sentence.

EXAMPLE:

The player used a **?** *to hit a homerun.*

By looking at the words around **?** we can tell that they are playing baseball and the baseball player hit a homerun using a **bat**.

Contraction

Two words joined together to make a shorter word using an apostrophe.

EXAMPLE:

cannot ~ can't   we are ~ we're   I am ~ I'm

Critical Thinking

To logically evaluate what is heard or read. To carefully examine the information for accuracy and recognize inconsistencies or contradictions. Test conclusions to ensure facts are backed up by evidence and eliminate faulty information.

Language Arts

Degree

Words (adjectives) that show a comparison between items. It can also make a statement about something such as a positive degree.

1. The positive degree simply describes something when there is **no comparison** being made.

EXAMPLE: August *is* a very hot month.

2. The comparative degree is used when comparing two things by adding *-er* to the adjective or using the word **more**.

EXAMPLE: August is *hotter* than May.

3. The superlative degree shows comparison of three or more things by adding *-est* to the adjective or using the word **most**.

EXAMPLE: August is the *hottest* month.

Denotation

The literal meaning of a given word.

EXAMPLE:

The denotation of the word *hurry* is to move quickly. Other words may have the same meaning. The words *rush* and *hurry* have the same meaning.

Language Arts

Dewey Decimal System

The system used by libraries to organize their books. There are 10 main categories or subject areas in the Dewey Decimal System.

000-099 **General Works** - includes reference materials

100-199 **Philosophy** - includes psychology

200-299 **Religion**

300-399 **Social Sciences** - education, economics law, sociology

400-499 **Language** - books, dictionaries, grammar

500-599 **Science** - astronomy, biology, chemistry, math, physics

600-699 **Technology** - computers, medicine, aviation, engineering

700-799 **Arts** - hobbies, music, painting, sports

800-899 **Literature** - plays, poetry, essays

900-999 **History** - biography, geography, travel

Each subject is assigned a particular area in the library within that category.

Language Arts

Dictionary

A book which gives the definition, pronunciation, origin of usage, and spelling of words. Here are the parts of the dictionary:

Definition

Gives the meaning of each word depending on the context in which it is used. Each word has at least one definition. If the word has multiple meanings then it will give each meaning and an example.

Entry Word

Entry words are shown in bold type and shows each word divided into syllables.

Guide Words

The words printed at the top of the page in a dictionary or encyclopedia. All the main entries which fall alphabetically between these two words will be on that page, guide words included.

Parts of Speech

Indicates whether the word is a noun, pronoun, adjective, verb, adverb, interjection, preposition, or a conjunction.

Pronunciation

The pronunciation of a word is given in parentheses next to the entry word. Letter symbols are used to show how a word sounds. The pronunciation key at the beginning of the dictionary gives examples of the sounds of each symbol.

Language Arts

Digraph (sh-ch-th-wh-gh-ph)
Two letters combined to make one sound.

EXAMPLES:

Shut, **Ch**eck, **Th**e, **Wh**en, Thou**gh**, **Ph**one

Diphthong
When two different vowels are next to each other in a
word and you can hear both vowels. This sound is
pronounced in one syllable.

EXAMPLES:

The **-ou** sound in the word h**ou**se or the **-oi** sound
in the word n**oi**se.

Encyclopedia
A set of books containing information on people,
places, things, and events.

Fantasy
Something that can exist only in the imagination.

EXAMPLE:

Superman is a fantasy because a flying man
doesn't exist in our world.

Language Arts

Fiction

Is something that is not true or real.

EXAMPLE:

Willie Wonka and the Chocolate Factory is fiction because it isn't true. *Independence Day* is a science fiction movie and *Apollo 13* is nonfiction because it really happened.

Figurative Language

Figurative language describes real items or events in an imaginative way. See similes, metaphors, personification, and idioms for specific examples.

Folk Tale

A story handed down through time from person to person. A folk tale starts out telling about real people but each time the story is told a new idea is added until it *can* become a myth. These folk tales can also be in the form of a song.

EXAMPLE:

Paul Bunyan and *The Fish Story* can be considered folk tales. The Fish Story is a good example of how the story changes over time.

Language Arts

Footnote

A footnote gives an explanation or the source of a quotation, fact, or idea that is used in your paper. Footnotes are indicated by a small raised number and are generally located at the bottom of the page or grouped together at the end of the chapter.

EXAMPLES:

Book (one author)

Author-Title-Edition-City of Publication-Year-Page #

[1]D. J. McLaughlin, <u>The Student's Homework Handbook</u> (2d ed; Poway: DAMAND Publishing, 2010), p. 513.

Book (two or more authors)

Authors-Title-Edition-City of Publication-Year-Page #

[2]D. J. McLaughlin and C. L. Davis, <u>The Parent's Homework Dictionary</u> (2d ed; Poway: DAMAND Publishing, 1996), p. 621.

Magazine

Title of Story-Magazine-Date of Issue-Page #

[3]"Bugs Bunny Wins the Championship," Newsmonth (November 10, 2001), p. 10.

Newspaper Article

Author-Title of Story-Newspaper-Date of Issue-Page #-Column

[4]Tomas Torres, "Yankees Win the World Series," <u>Imperial Valley Press</u> (December 26, 2007), p.13, col 2.

Language Arts

Foreshadowing

Hints or suggestions about what's to come in a story. We look at the setting, mood, characters actions and words, and any other information or foreshadowing from the story in order to make a predication.

Homograph

Word that is spelled the same but has a different meaning and pronunciation.

EXAMPLE:

Please *lead* the class to lunch.
The *lead* in my pencil broke during the test.

Homonym

Word that is spelled the same but has a different meaning.

EXAMPLE:

To eat a *mint* (candy) is different than the gold is kept at the *mint*.

Homophone

Words that sound alike but have different spellings and meanings.

EXAMPLES:

wear-where; loan-lone; hear-here

Language Arts

Idiom or Idiomatic Phrase

A phrase that has a special meaning and cannot be taken literally.

EXAMPLE:

Idiom: *It is raining cats and dogs.*

The idiom **raining cats and dogs** means it is raining very hard. Idioms cannot be understood just by the individual words and generally cannot be directly translated into another language.

Inference

When only some of the facts are given inference can find the missing information. Often times a mystery story won't give you all the information so you have to infer (guess) the missing information.

EXAMPLE:

Inference

Melissa placed the worm on the hook and then placed the hook in the water. After awhile she felt a tug on her line so she reeled it in and took a look at her hook but nothing was there.

Fishing was never mentioned in the sentences but we know that Melissa was fishing.

Language Arts

Interjection

Word or group of words that express feeling or emotion and are generally set apart from the sentence by an exclamation point (strong emotions) or a comma. An interjection usually appears at the beginning of a sentence.

Common Interjections:

Ah, Good grief, Hey, Hurrah, Oh, Oh no, Oops, Ouch, Ugh, Whew, Wow

EXAMPLE:

Wow! That was a great game.

Interjection: *Wow*

EXAMPLE:

Hey, look before you cross the street!

Interjection: *Hey*

Metaphor

Compares two unlike things by stating that one thing *is* another.

EXAMPLE:

Our teacher *is* a computer when she adds.

Metaphor: *teacher ~ computer*

This means that the teacher is very good at addition.

Language Arts

Modifier (*adjectives*)
A modifier describes words (nouns) in a sentence.

EXAMPLE:

The *striped* shirt was torn in the wash.

Modifier: *striped*

Myth
Are stories from ancient times that tell about the adventures and great courage of gods, goddesses, and superheroes. Hercules would be considered a myth.

Negative
A word meaning *no* or *not*. Contractions using the word *not* are also considered negatives.

EXAMPLES:

We *won't* be able to go to the zoo.

Negative: *won't*

You are *not* allowed to go to the game.

Negative: *not*

Language Arts

Nonfiction

Books containing factual information. A history book is an example of nonfiction.

Noun

Names a person, place, thing, or idea in a given sentence.

EXAMPLE:

Jennifer read a *book* about *college*.

Nouns: *Jennifer, book, college*

Noun - collective

Refers to a group of animals, people, or things in a sentence. *Group, crowd, class, family, team* are all collective nouns.

EXAMPLES:

The *family* went to the beach.

Collective Noun: *family*

Will the *team* drive with us?

Collective Noun: *team*

The *class* won a trip to Washington.

Collective Noun: *class*

Language Arts

Noun - compound

Two or more words used as a single noun. Compound nouns can be written as a single, separate, or hyphenated word.

EXAMPLES:

New York, son-in-law, baseball are all compound nouns.

Noun - plural

Names <u>more than</u> one person, place, thing, or idea.

EXAMPLES:

1. Nouns ending in **s, ch, x,** or **sh**... add **-es** (glas<u>s</u> ~ glas<u>ses</u>; ben<u>ch</u> ~ ben<u>ches</u>; a<u>x</u> ~ a<u>xes</u>; fini<u>sh</u> ~ finis<u>hes</u>)

2. Nouns ending with a vowel and **y**... add **-s** (valley ~ valley<u>s</u>)

3. Nouns ending with a consonant and **y**... change the *y* to *i* and add **-es** (city~ci<u>ties</u>)

4. Nouns ending in *f* or *fe*... change the *f* to *v* and add **-es** to some words and just add **-s** to others (lea<u>f</u> ~ lea<u>ves</u>; cliff ~ cliff<u>s</u>)

Language Arts

Noun - plural continued

5. Nouns ending with a vowel and **o**... add **-s**
   (rad<u>lo</u> ~ radio<u>s</u>)

6. Nouns ending with a consonant and **o**... add
   -es to some words and **-s** to others
   (he<u>ro</u> ~ hero<u>es</u>; pian<u>o</u> ~ piano<u>s</u>)

7. Most singular nouns just add **-s** except for
   special words such as *foot ~ feet* and
   woman ~ women

Noun - plural possessive

A plural noun showing ownership. When the plural
noun ends in *-s* add an apostrophe to the end of the
word (s').

EXAMPLE:

*The cars that belong to the players are parked in the
parking lot.*

Change to:
The **players'** cars are parked in the parking lot.

Plural Possessive Noun: players'

For plural nouns that ***do not*** end in *-s* add an
apostrophe *s* ('s) to make it a possessive noun
(mice ~ mice's).

Language Arts

Noun - proper

Names an *individual* (particular) noun like the name of a river.

EXAMPLE:

The word *river* would be a common noun while the *Colorado River* would be a proper noun.

Noun - singular possessive

Shows ownership by adding an *apostrophe* and *-s* ('s) to the end of the word.

EXAMPLE:

The tiger has big teeth.

Change to: The *tiger's* teeth are big.

Singular Possessive Noun: *tiger's*

Objects - direct

Follows the action verb in a sentence. The direct object is a noun or pronoun in the predicate that receives the action of the verb from the subject.

EXAMPLE:

The boy steers the red *bike*.

Subject: boy

Verb: steers

Direct Object: *bike*

Language Arts

Object - indirect

The direct object receives the action while the indirect object tells who or what receives the action. The indirect object can come between the **verb** and **direct object** or at the end of he sentence.

EXAMPLES:

    (s)   (v)   (D.O.)   (I.O.)

The pitcher threw the ball to the *catcher*.

Subject: pitcher (s)

Action Verb: threw (v)

Direct Object: ball (D.O.)

Indirect Object: *catcher* (I.O.)

Onomatopoeia

The use of words that imitate or copy sounds.

EXAMPLE:

To say *rrrrrrrace* car would sound like the revving of a race car engine.

To say that an engine *purrrrrrrred* would mean that the engine was running in a smooth and quiet manner.

Language Arts

Outlining

There are several outline patterns, however, the example given below is the most common outline used in our school system.

1. Begin your outline with a title for the subject.

2. Arrange your main topics in a logical order.

3. Use Roman numerals in front of the main topics:
I-II-III-IV-V-VI and so on.

4. Use capital letters for each subtopic.

5. Use Arabic numbers for each detail.

Rules
If you have a **I** then you have to have a **II**, if you have an **A** there has to be a **B**, etc. Capitalize the first word in each main topic, subtopic, and detail.

Writing using the outline
It is easier to get your learner to write an outline then it is to write a paper. However, once they organize their thoughts it is very easy to write a paper. Look at the sample outline on the next page of Michael Jordan (detail). Once they write several details about a subtopic the rest is easy!

Sample Sentences:
Michael Jordan is one of the greatest basketball players ever! He has helped the Bulls win five championships in the last six years. He has also been an all-star 10 times and he has won the scoring title seven times.

Three sentences just from one detail!

Language Arts

Outlining sample

Sports Greatest Teams

(Title of Subject)

Main Topic **I. Basketball**

    Subtopic   **A.** *Chicago Bulls*

        Detail   **1. Michael Jordan**
        Detail   **2. Bob Love**

    Subtopic   **B.** *Boston Celtics*

        Detail   **1. Larry Bird**
        Detail   **2. Bill Russell**

Main Topic **II. Baseball**

    Subtopic   **A.** *Los Angeles Dodgers*

        Detail   **1. Steve Garvey**
        Detail   **2. Sandy Koufax**

    Subtopic   **B.** *New York Yankees*

        Detail   **1. Mickey Mantle**
        Detail   **2. Lou Gehrig**

Main Topic **III. Football**

    Subtopic   **A.** *Oakland Raiders*

        Detail   **1. Kenny Stabler**
        Detail   **2. Marcus Allen**

    Subtopic   **D.** *Miami Dolphins*

        Detail   **1. Dan Marino**
        Detail   **2. Bob Grease**

Just continue to follow the format!

Language Arts

Overgeneralization

A very broad statement that does not follow the facts.

EXAMPLE:

Our teacher said that she liked basketball.

A good example of overgeneralization would be to say that **all teachers like basketball**. This cannot be determined from the information on just one teacher!

Paragraph & Supporting Details

A group of sentences telling about the same idea. Each paragraph should have a topic sentence and supporting details. The main idea should be supported by the sentences in the paragraph.

EXAMPLE:

The aircraft carrier *Enterprise* is one of the largest ships in our navy. *This floating giant* can carry as many as 100 aircraft and over 5,000 men. The top speed of this *massive ship* is over 30 miles per hour. *It* generates enough electricity to light a city. On any given day more than 3,000 hamburgers, 2,000 eggs, and 1,000 hotdogs are eaten *on board ship*.

Main Idea: *The Enterprise*

Language Arts

Paragraph & Supporting Details   continued

Supporting Details:

*large ship

*carry as many as **100** aircraft and over **5,000**
   men

*top speed over **30** miles per hour

*generates enough electricity to light a city

***3,000** hamburgers, **2,000** eggs, and **1,000**
   hotdogs are eaten

When writing a paragraph on any subject all you
need to do is organize your main ideas and
supporting details. Once you organize your ideas
use descriptive words to describe the details. For
example, instead of saying: *"This ship goes fast"*

we said

*"The top speed of this massive ship is over 30 miles
per hour."*

Whioh sentence do you prefer?

Language Arts

Participle
Verb form that can function as either a verb or adjective.

EXAMPLES:

Verb	Present Participle	Past	Past Participle
paint	is painting	painted	has painted
plan	is planning	planned	has planned
play	is playing	played	has played

Parts of Speech (see individual words for examples)

Adjective
A word that tells what kind, how many, or which one.

Adverb
A word that tells where, when, how, or how much.

Conjunction
A word that connects words or a group of words.

Interjection
A word that expresses a strong feeling and is set apart from the sentence by a comma or exclamation point.

Language Arts

Parts of Speech continued

Noun
A word that names a person, place, idea, or thing.

Preposition
A word that shows a relationship between a noun and another word in the sentence.

Pronoun
A word that takes the place of a noun or nouns.

Verb
A word that shows action or links the subject to a word or phrase that tells about the subject.

Personification
Gives objects human qualities.

EXAMPLES:

The computer has a mind of its own.

The car is being stubborn!

The computer really doesn't have a mind and a car can't be stubborn.

Language Arts

Poetry

Haiku is a short Japanese poem. Haiku usually follows a pattern of three lines with seventeen syllables. The first line has five syllables, the second line has seven, and the third line has five.

Limerick is a nonsense poem that has five lines of special rhymes or rhythm schemes.

Sonnet is a fourteen line poem of a set rhyme scheme and movement.

Repetition is simply repeating words or phrases over and over again. This type of poem is designed to emphasize the main idea and assist the reader in remembering that idea.

Predicate

Tells what the subject is or what it does (the verb).
Hint: Look for the action word most of the time!

EXAMPLE:

The driver **steers** the big bus.

Subject: *driver*

Predicate: *steers*

Language Arts

Predicate - complete
All the words that make up the predicate.

EXAMPLE:

The capital of Texas is Austin.

Complete Predicate: *is Austin*

Predicate - compound
When two or more simple predicates are combined in a sentence using a conjunction (and/or). Combine the two simple predicates in the following sentences:

EXAMPLE:

The girls stood at the game.
The girls watched the game.
The girls *stood and watched* the game.

Compound Predicate: *stood and watched*

Prefix
Letters added to the beginning of words to change the meaning or tense.

EXAMPLES:

re ~ make   **re**make
un ~ known   **un**known
dis ~ like   **dis**like

Language Arts

Preposition

Word that shows the relationship (where something is at) between a noun or pronoun and other words in the sentence.

EXAMPLE:

Lisa found the book *under* the chair.

Preposition: *under*

Preposition - object of the

Noun or pronoun that follows the preposition.

EXAMPLE:

Billy found the book under the *chair*.

Object of the Preposition: *chair*

Under is the preposition because it shows a relationship between Billy and the chair. So, *chair* must be the object of the preposition.

Prepositional Phrase

Is made up of the preposition, the object of the preposition, and all the words in between.

EXAMPLE:

Billy found the book *under the chair*.

Preposition: *under*
Object of the Preposition: *chair*
Prepositional Phrase: *under the chair*

Language Arts

Pronoun

A word that takes the place of a noun or nouns.
Pronouns include *I*, *we*, *they*, *she*, *he*, *you*, *me*,
it, *us*, *them*, *him*, and *her*.

EXAMPLES:

Miss McMahan went to the restaurant yesterday.
She went to the restaurant yesterday.

Pronoun: *She*
She replaces the name *Miss McMahan*.

Al and *Peggy* went to the beach yesterday.
They went to the beach yesterday.

Pronoun: *They*
They replaces the names *Al* and *Peggy*.

Pronoun - object

Can replace nouns used ***after*** verbs or ***after*** words
such as: *to, for, with, in, at.*

Object Pronouns: *me, you, he, her, it, us, them*

EXAMPLE:

Lisa waved *to* the *crowd.*
Lisa waved *to* **them.**

Verb: *waved*
Object Pronoun: *them*

Language Arts

Pronoun - possessive

A possessive pronoun can replace a possessive noun. Some possessive pronouns appear before a noun. Use *my, your, his, her, its, our,* and *their* before nouns in a sentence.

EXAMPLES:

His story will be printed in the newspaper.

Possessive Pronoun: *His*

Please give back *my* baseball.

Possessive Pronoun: *my*

That ball is *mine*!

Possessive Pronoun: *mine*

Our car has a dent in the fender.

Possessive Pronoun: *Our*

Punctuation

Apostrophes (') - Are used to form possessive singular nouns (teacher's), plural nouns that end in -s (Torres'), plural nouns that don't end in -s (women's), and in contractions to replace dropped letters (they will ~ they'll).

End Marks - At the end of a sentence. A period (.) ends a declarative or imperative sentence, a question mark (?) ends a question, and an exclamation point (!) ends an exclamation.

Language Arts

Punctuation continued

Colon (:) - Can be used after a greeting in a business letter, before a list, or to join two complete sentences.

Comma (,) - see Comma

Quotation Marks (" ") - Used to show a person's exact words.

Semicolon (;) - A strong comma to separate phrases, titles, or names with addresses.

Quotation

Direct - Gives a speakers exact words. Exact quotes are capitalized and have quotation marks at the beginning and end of the quote.

EXAMPLE:

"Always do your best," said the teacher.

Indirect - States what a person said without using their exact words.

EXAMPLE:

The teacher said to do our best.

Language Arts

Sentence
A group of words that express a complete thought. The sentence must contain a subject and a predicate.

EXAMPLE:

subject   predicate
Elmo likes to be tickled on the tummy.

Sentence - declarative
Makes a statement and ends with a period.

EXAMPLE:

The first day of practice is always the hardest.

Sentence - exclamatory
Expresses strong feelings and ends with an exclamation point.

EXAMPLE:

She is a great mom!

Sentence - imperative
Gives a command or makes a request and ends with a period.

EXAMPLE:

Don't run on the bus. Please check your binder.

Language Arts

Sentence - fragment
A group of words that do not express a complete thought or does not have a subject and/or a predicate.

EXAMPLE:

Complete Sentence:
Kermit and Miss Piggy *went to the beach*.

Sentence Fragment: *went to the beach*

The words do not make a complete sentence because the subject (who or what) is missing.

Sentence - interrogative
Asks a question and ends with a question mark.

EXAMPLE:

When will Mandy arrive from college**?**

Simile
Compares two things by stating that one item *is like* another.

EXAMPLE:

The **runner** runs **like** the **wind**.

Simile: runner ~ wind

This just means that the runner is fast.

Language Arts

Subject
Tells whom or what the sentence is about.

EXAMPLE:

The *tiger* slept all day.

Subject: *tiger*   **Predicate:** slept

Hint - Look for the noun doing the action!

Subject - complete
All the words (modifiers) that make up the subject.
Include both subjects (coach & quarterback) and all
the words in between!

EXAMPLE:

The *coach and the quarterback* waved to the crowd.

Complete Subject:
coach and the quarterback

Subject - simple
The most important word or words in the complete
subject.

EXAMPLE:

The *coach* and the *quarterback* waved to the
crowd.

Complete Subject: *coach and the quarterback*

Simple Subject: *coach & quarterback*

Language Arts

Subject ~ Verb Agreement

When there is a *singular* subject there must be a *singular* verb. When there is a *plural* subject there must be a *plural* verb. This means the subject and verb agree in number.

EXAMPLES:

The <u>student</u> <u>is</u> a fast runner.
The <u>students</u> <u>are</u> fast runner<u>s</u>.

<u>He</u> <u>is</u> a fast runner.
<u>They</u> <u>are</u> fast runner<u>s</u>.

<u>Ms. Jones</u> <u>is</u> a good teacher.
<u>Mr. Mac</u> and <u>Ms. Jones</u> <u>are</u> good teacher<u>s</u>.

<u>Uncle Woodrow</u> <u>was</u> a WWII hero.
<u>Uncle Woodrow</u> and <u>Dr. Gaynor</u> <u>were</u> WWII hero<u>es</u>.

Subordinate Clause

A *subordinate clause* will begin with a subordinate conjunction or a relative pronoun and contain both a subject and a verb. This group of words will not form a complete sentence. It will instead leave the reader wanting more information.

Subordinate Conjunctions: *after, although, because, if, once, until, while, etc.*

EXAMPLE: After *Bob* threw the ball.........

Subject: *Bob*
Predicate: *threw*

Language Arts

Suffix
A suffix is added to the end of a base word.

EXAMPLE:

		base word suffix
wearable	=	wear ~ *able*
basement	=	base ~ *ment*
played	=	play ~ *ed*

Summarizing
A way of condensing information using only the key points. The opening sentence should give a clear description of the main idea. The rest of the summary should support the main idea in as few words as possible without changing the meaning. The summary must be in sequence with the story.

1. Tell about the main setting, characters, and the plot.

2. State any major conflicts and how that conflict came into being a conflict.

3. Finish with how the story or movie ended and how the conflict was solved.

Language Arts

Syllabication

A way of dividing words into syllables usually seen in dictionaries.

EXAMPLE: syl-lab-i-ca-tion

Rules: *For dividing words into syllables.*

1. Affixes

When a word has an affix (prefix or suffix) divide between the root word and affix:
Prefix: **re ~ write**   *Suffix:* **help ~ ful**

2. Compound Words

Divide between the two words: **foot ~ ball**

3. Double Consonants

When a word has double consonants divide between the double consonants: **bub ~ ble**

4. Two Consonants

When two consonants are between two vowels divide between the consonants: **sis ~ ter**

5. One Consonant

When one consonant is between two vowels divide the word between the first vowel and the consonant: **spo ~ ken**

Language Arts

Syllabication continued

6. Ending in LE
When a consonant is followed by -LE divide
the word before the consonant: **ta ~ ble**

7. X
When the letter x is between two vowels
divide the word after the x: **ox ~ en**

Synonym
Words that have similar meaning.

EXAMPLE:

The word *__talk__* has the following synonyms:

Please *speak* to the teacher.
Please *yell* to the teacher.
Please *relate* to the teacher.
Please *explain* to the teacher.
Please *convey* to the teacher.

Tense - future
A verb that tells what will happen in the future by
using the helping verbs *will* or *shall*.

EXAMPLES:

Elaine *will* bring her new car to the parade.

Future Tense: *will*

Language Arts

Tense - past

A verb that shows what has already happened.

EXAMPLE:

Stephanie *liked* her grandmother's pie.

Past Tense: *liked*

Rules: (For forming past tense)

1. Most verbs add *-ed* (play-played)

2. Verbs ending with *e*...add *-d* (hope-hoped)

3. Verbs ending with a consonant and *y* change the *y* to *i* and add *-ed* (study-studied)

4. Verbs ending with a single vowel and a consonant just double the final consonant and add *-ed* (stop-stopped)

Tense - present

A verb that shows action as it is happening.

EXAMPLE: The teacher *sees* the students.

Present Tense: *sees*

Rules: (For forming present tense)
Add *-s* when the verb is singular and do not change the verb with plural subject or with the pronouns *I* and *you*.

Language Arts

Titles

The first, last, and all the important words capitalized in the title. Printed titles of books, magazines, newspapers, and movies should appear in italics or underlined. Quotation marks should be used for songs, articles, book chapters, poems, and titles of short stories. Do not capitalize words such as: *the, a, in, and, or of,* unless they begin or end the title.

EXAMPLE: Movie Title

Return of the Jedi

Topic

The subject of each sentence, paragraph, or story. Each sentence will have a topic (subject).

EXAMPLE:

The *tiger* is a large and beautiful animal. However, you would not want *one* as a house cat. *It* can weigh several hundred pounds and can eat $40 of meat each day.

Topic: *tiger*

Because each sentence tells something about a tiger.

Language Arts

Topic Sentence and Main Idea

The first sentence that best describes the main idea of a paragraph. The topic sentence is then supported by details.

EXAMPLE: *Read the following paragraph*

The aircraft carrier Constellation is one of the largest ships in our navy. It can carry up to 100 aircraft and over 5,000 men. The top speed of this massive ship is over 30 miles per hour. It can also generate enough electricity to light a city.

Main Idea: Constellation

Topic Sentence:
The aircraft carrier Constellation is one of the largest ships in our navy.

The rest of the supporting sentences tell something about the Constellation!

Verb

Action word that tells what the subject does or did.
Hint: Look for action words or helping verbs!

EXAMPLE:

The ball *flew* over the fence.

Subject: *ball*
Verb: *flew*

Language Arts

Verb - helping or auxiliary

Works with the main verb to form a verb phrase. Helping verbs do not show action.

EXAMPLE:

Mandy *is* winning the race.

Helping Verb: *is*

Common Helping Verbs:
has-have; is-are; will-shall; must-ought;
can-could; should-would; do-did

Verb - irregular

Verbs that *do not* need *-d* or *-ed* to show that something has already happened.

EXAMPLES:

Verb ~ *Irregular Verb*

bring ~ *brought*	come ~ *came*
go ~ *went*	make ~ *made*
run ~ *ran*	say ~ *said*
take ~ *took*	think ~ *thought*
write ~ *wrote*	ring ~ *rang*
sing ~ *sang*	swim ~ *swam*
begin ~ *began*	tear ~ *tore*
wear ~ *wore*	break ~ *broke*
speak ~ *spoke*	steal ~ *stole*
choose ~ *chose*	freeze ~ *froze*
blow ~ *blew*	grow ~ *grew*
know ~ *knew*	fly ~ *flew*

Language Arts

Verb - linking

Links the subject of the sentence with a word or words in the predicate. A linking verb does not show action and is not a helping verb. It is also followed by a word in the predicate that names or describes the subject.

EXAMPLE:

Jenny *was* a <u>teacher</u>.

Linking Verb: *was*

Common Linking Verbs: am, was, are, is, were, be, look, feel, taste, smell, seem, appear

Verb Phrases

Made up of a main verb and a helping verb.

EXAMPLE:

Mandy *is winning* the race.

Verb Phrase: *is winning*

Verb - regular

Shows past tense by adding *-d* or *-ed* to the end of the word.

EXAMPLES:
jump ~ jumped   leap ~ leaped   type ~ typed

Language Arts

Verb - transitive

When <u>someone</u> or <u>something</u> in the predicate receives that action.

EXAMPLE:

The students ***cheered*** the *principal*.

Transitive Verb: ***cheered***

Direct Object: *principal*
(the principal received the action)

Vowel Rules

Most words in the English language follow rules just like students follow rules in their classroom. Vowels and consonants are put together to make words. The words are sounded out by where each vowel and consonant is placed in that word. If you follow the rules below it will help you sound out most words in our language.

C stands for consonant
V stands for vowel

1. CVVC

When two vowels are together you hear only the first long vowel sound.

Example: ^{c v v c} **meat**

Language Arts

2. VCV

When a consonant is between two vowels and the last vowel is an -e the first vowel has a long vowel sound.

Example: ^{v c v} **ate**

3. VCCCV

When two or more consonants are between two vowels the first vowel has a short vowel sound.

Example: ^{v c c c v} **apple**

4. CVC

When a vowel is between two consonants the vowel sound is short.

Example: ^{c v c} **cup**

5. CV

When a vowel follows a consonant in a two letter word the vowel is long.

Example: ^{c v} **so**

Language Arts

Word Connotations

A word that suggests meaning in addition to its definition. Connotations can be positive, negative, or neutral.

EXAMPLE:

Kenny Stabler threw a long pass that was dropped in the end zone and we just sat there, *marveling*.

The word *marveling* could mean:

1. Marveling can have a ***positive*** meaning in that we were delighted at the dropped pass.

2. It can have a ***negative*** meaning in that we were staring in displeasure at the dropped pass.

3. It can also have a ***neutral*** meaning in that we just watched the event.

Writing Process

Prewriting

Done before any writing takes place. Brainstorm a list of ideas about the topic. Use this list to discuss ideas with fellow classmates. Once a list has been decided upon gather information on the items/subject. Consider the audience that will read or hear your words. This will assist you in using the correct vocabulary for the audience.

Language Arts

Drafting

Organize your thoughts on paper. Place the ideas in a logical sequence and develop each one to write a first draft. Have others read your paper and offer suggestions.

Revising

This is the time to improve on original ideas. Rearrange your ideas and words to fit the writing and take out or add parts that will help make it a better paper. Complete any unfinished ideas and replace overused or unclear words.

Proofreading

Examine the paper for grammar and punctuation. Look for words that are used out of context or incorrectly. After these corrections are made have someone read it again. Copy it again, making all the corrections. Make sure it is a neat paper!

Publishing

Now you can share your final paper. Remember, neatness counts! Bind your work so that it is appealing. Illustrate the cover or different parts so that the reader can better understand the story. Always remember that mental image you want your readers to have of your writing.

Language Arts

Writing (parts of a story)

Plot
Beginning - State the opening problem
Middle - State the consequences of the problem
End - State how the problem was solved

Setting
The time and the place of the story. Provide
clues for the reader to make conclusions or
be descriptive. Give a mood of the characters
or their surroundings.

Characters
Can be animals, people, or imaginary beings.

Writing Made Easy
Believe it or not, writing can be easy if we follow two
simple rules.

1. Make the sentences interesting, relevant,
    and in sequence.

2. Organize your thoughts in sequence and in
    the given format (summary, biography,
    story, etc.).

Here is the assignment: Have your child write a
paragraph about what they did this weekend. How
much will they write?????

Language Arts

EXAMPLE:

I went to the movies with my friend.   My family went out to dinner Saturday night.   I played a game with my brother.   We went to grandma's house Sunday morning.

Have you seen this style of writing before? Some students may have difficulty expressing themselves in writing. Writing is hard work to them but maybe we can do something to give the paper feeling and make it easier. Now let's take a look at this paragraph one sentence at a time. We will add some colorful words (adjectives and adverbs) to make each sentence more interesting so that the reader will have a mental image of the writing.

Sentence One:
I went to the movies with my friend.

How about this instead:

Bobby and *I* went to see a **fantastic** movie Friday night. The movie was about **aliens** from another planet **trying to take over the world** and it was called **Independence Day**.

Difference:
We now have two sentences telling the reader who went to the movie, what they saw, the plot, and how they felt about the movie (fantastic).

Language Arts

Sentence Two:
My family went out to dinner Saturday night.

How about this instead:

After a ***long day of shopping*** on Saturday my family went to eat ***hamburgers*** at ***Crustiburgers***. The ***hamburgers*** were ***good*** but the ***fries*** were ***cold***!

Difference:
Now we know that the writer didn't like his/her day of shopping (long day), what and where they ate, and a description of the food.

Sentence Three:
I played a video game with my brother.

How about this instead:

After we got home my brother wanted to play a video game. He ***bothered me for 30 minutes*** until I finally said okay. We played a quick game of football and ***I beat him 13-10***.

Difference:
The writer really didn't want to play a game. However, he/she did play football and won.

Language Arts

Sentence Four:
We went to grandma's house Sunday morning.

How about this instead:

We got up *early* Sunday morning and went to grandma's house.

Difference:
This new sentence tells the reader the time of day (early).

New Paragraph:

Bobby and I went to see a fantastic movie Friday night. The movie was about aliens from another planet trying to take over the world and it was called *Independence Day*. After a long day of shopping on Saturday my family went to eat hamburgers at Crustiburgers. The hamburgers were good but the fries were cold! After we got home my brother wanted to play a video game. He bothered me for 30 minutes until I finally said okay. We played a quick game of football and I beat him 13-10. We got up early Sunday morning and went to grandma's house.

This is *not* a perfect paragraph but notice how much more we have in the way of length and description!

Math

Addition   72

Subtraction   78

Multiplication   84

Division   90

Fractions   98

Decimals   114

Geometry   120

Algebra   129

General Terms   153

Addition

Addition Definitions

Addend

One of two or more numbers added together to find a sum.

EXAMPLE:

$$2 + 3 = 5$$

The digits 2 and 3 are addends.

Digit

Make sure to emphasize the difference between a digit and a number. A digit is just one place in a number. There are three digits in the <u>number</u> **175**.

175 = the digit *1*, the digit *7*, the digit *5*

Sum

When numbers are added together their total (answer) is called the sum.

EXAMPLE:

$$2 + 2 = 4$$

4 is the sum

Addition

There are many ways to introduce the concept of addition. Here are a few ways to help your learner understand the process.

Introduction: Let's use baseballs to introduce the concept of addition. Once the child understands this concept we can match this to a mathematical expression (sentence).

EXAMPLE:

$$1 \quad + \quad 2 \quad = \quad 3$$

Note: Kids like to use their fingers in the beginning stages of learning addition and subtraction. Use whatever works to get the point across.

Hint: Once your child understands addition, use different items such as marbles, pennies, different colored items, or boys and girls to reinforce their new knowledge. If you allow gum or candy in your home this is always an effective way to get their attention!

For Advanced Learners

Another way to get the point across is to divide a group of items in half and make an addition problem.

$\quad 3 + 3 = 6$

This is a great way to introduce the concept of division and multiplication. $3 \times 2 = 6 \quad 6 \div 2 = 3$ etc.

Addition

Another Hint: This is a good time to use pennies because this would introduce the value of money and at the same time create interest in this concept (addition). We can also add two weeks together 7 + 7. This will reinforce the number of days in a week.

Adding Multiple Digit Numbers

When adding multiple digit numbers write the math problem in columns. Since we are introducing this concept it would be a good idea to label each place value.

It is easier for students to add when the numbers are stacked in columns (vertical format). Just remember to add two digits (one column) at a time starting with the column at the right (ones)!

EXAMPLE:

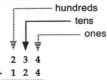

Add the ones, then the tens, then the hundreds column, etc.

```
    2 3 4        2 3 4        2 3 4
  + 1 2 4      + 1 2 4      + 1 2 4
  ───────      ───────      ───────
        8          5 8      3 5 8
```

Addition

Problem Area

It helps some learners to cover up the digits except for the ones being added together. Here is how our addition problem looks if we cover the numbers <u>not</u> being added.

Addition problem

```
    2  3  4
 +  1  2  4
```

Step One　　　　**4**　*first, add the ones column*
```
 +       4
 ────────
         8
```

Step Two　　　**3** 4　*second, add the tens column*
```
 +    2  4
 ────────
      5  8
```

Step Three　　**2** 3 4　*now, the hundreds column*
```
 +  1  2  4
 ────────
    3  5  8
```

This will help our learners breakdown a large scary problem into smaller, more manageable parts. Seeing large numbers for the first time can be intimidating!

Hint: By only adding (and seeing) two digits at a time our learners can grasp this concept more easily. If we use this same process for subtraction, multiplication, or division our learners will feel more comfortable and confident through the entire problem.

Addition

Adding *(regrouping)*

When adding two or more digits and the total is more than nine we need to regroup. We take the tens digit and add it to the next column.

Rules: Just follow these steps when explaining the process. It is important to follow the correct order at all times!

Step One: Add the ones together

Step Two: Regroup if necessary by carrying over the 10's digit to the next column

Step Three: Add the entire tens column

Step Four: Regroup if necessary by carrying over the digit to the hundreds column (for larger numbers)

Step Five: Add the entire hundreds column

EXAMPLE: Remember to add one column at a time starting with the ones!

$$
\begin{array}{r}
2\ 5 \\
+\ 2\ 7 \\
\end{array}
$$

Step One
$$
\begin{array}{r}
2\ 5 \\
+\ 2\ 7 \\
\hline
\underline{1}\ 2 \\
\end{array}
$$
5 + 7 = 12 so we have to carry the 1 to the tens place value and regroup (add)

Step Two
$$
\begin{array}{r}
\text{---▶ +1} \\
2\ 5 \\
+\ 2\ 7 \\
\hline
\bigcirc 2 \\
\end{array}
$$

Step Three
$$
\begin{array}{r}
+1 \\
2\ 5 \\
+\ 2\ 7 \\
\hline
5\ 2 \\
\end{array}
$$
now just add the tens column
1 + 2 + 2 = 5

76

Addition

Subtraction to check addition

Remember that subtraction is the opposite of addition and we can use subtraction to check an addition problem.

EXAMPLE:

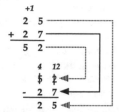

Hint: This is an excellent way for our learners to reinforce their subtraction skills at the same time prepare them for when they have to use more than one *operation* in a math problem. Meaning that there will be several functions in one equation. Such as addition, subtraction, multiplication, or division in the same equation. *See Order of Operation*

EXAMPLE:

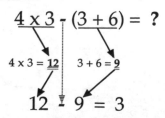

$$4 \times 3 - (3 + 6) = \ ?$$

$$4 \times 3 = \underline{12} \qquad 3 + 6 = \underline{9}$$

$$12 - 9 = 3$$

Subtraction

Subtraction Definitions

Minuend

The number being subtracted <u>from</u> is the *minuend*.

$$5 - 3 = 2$$

minuend

Subtrahend

The number <u>being</u> subtracted is the *subtrahend*.

$$5 - 3 = 2$$

subtrahend

Difference or *Remainder*

The new number left after the subtraction is complete
is called the *difference* or *remainder*.

$$5 - 3 = 2$$

difference

Subtraction

How to Subtract

Use any items that *grab* your learners attention. An interesting item could be dollar bills. So that is what we will use to introduce subtraction.

You start with five - $1 bills	$1 $1 $1 $1 $1
Now have your <u>learner</u> take $2	— $1 $1
This is how many you have left	$1 $1 $1

Do this several times with less than $10. Once our learner has a grasp of this concept put it in writing.

$$\$5 - \$2 = \$3$$

Hint: Just like with addition, when we introduce this concept it is important to use items (manipulatives) of interest to our learner.

Mental Math: Ask your learner how much they would have left if they started with $9 and bought a toy for $2. Kids will use a mental picture to come up with an answer.

Note: Often times subtraction is referred to as the difference between two numbers. The difference between 5 & 2 is 3. Another way to look at this problem is how far is it from 2 to 5? Counting from 2 to 5 is a total of 3 or the difference!

Subtraction

Subtracting multiple digit numbers (sentence form)

Use the following steps for this problem:

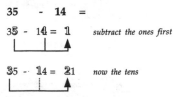

$$35 \quad - \quad 14 \quad =$$

35 - 14 = 1   *subtract the ones first*

35 - 14 = 21   *now the tens*

When **no** borrowing is involved this procedure should be easy. However, this is a more difficult procedure when we borrow.

Subtracting multiple digit numbers (column form)

In column form we proceed in the same manner as addition. One column at time!

EXAMPLE:

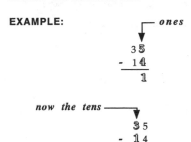

```
        ┌── ones
        ▼
    3 5
  - 1 4
  ─────
      1
```

now the tens ─────▼
```
    3 5
  - 1 4
  ─────
    2 1
```

Subtraction

Subtracting (borrowing)

At times, to solve a problem, borrowing is necessary. Remember, always subtract one column at a time and start with the ones!

    7 3   We can't take 5 away from 3 so
- 5 5   we borrow **one** from the 7.

Our 7 becomes 6   6 13

    7 3   *Our 3 becomes 13, now take*
- 5 5   *5 away from 13.* **Now the tens!**
  1 8

Because 5 is larger than 3 we can't take 5 away from 3. The 3 has to borrow from its neighbor the 7, in the tens place value, in order to have enough. The 3 becomes 13 and the 7 becomes 6.

This is how our subtraction problem would look if it were broken down one column at a time.

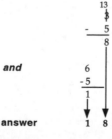

and

answer

81

Subtraction

Problem Area *Subtracting with multiple zeros*
This is a problem area because the usual *"borrowing from the neighbor"* rule becomes more complicated. We have to borrow from the neighbor that has money, so to speak.

EXAMPLE: 400 *We can't take 5 from 0 and when*
          − 275 *we look to the neighbor in the tens column we find another 0 so we can't borrow, yet. We have to move over to the hundreds column.*

$$
\begin{array}{r}
{\scriptstyle 3\ \ 10} \\
\cancel{4}0\,0 \\
-\ 2\,7\,5 \\
\hline
\end{array}
$$
The tens will first borrow from the hundreds.

$$
\begin{array}{r}
{\scriptstyle 9} \\
{\scriptstyle 3\ \ \cancel{10}\ \ 10} \\
\cancel{4}00 \\
-\ 275 \\
\hline
\end{array}
$$
Now our ones can borrow from the tens.

$$
\begin{array}{r}
{\scriptstyle 9} \\
{\scriptstyle 3\ \ \cancel{10}\ \ 10} \\
\cancel{4}\,\cancel{0}\,\cancel{0} \\
-\ 2\,7\,5 \\
\hline
5
\end{array}
$$
<u>*5 subtracted from 10 = 5*</u>

$$
\begin{array}{r}
{\scriptstyle 9} \\
{\scriptstyle 3\ \ \cancel{10}\ \ 10} \\
\cancel{4}\,\cancel{0}\,\cancel{0} \\
-\ 2\,7\,5 \\
\hline
2\,5
\end{array}
$$
<u>*7 subtracted from 9 = 2*</u>

$$
\begin{array}{r}
{\scriptstyle 9} \\
{\scriptstyle 3\ \ \cancel{10}\ \ 10} \\
\cancel{4}\,\cancel{0}\,\cancel{0} \\
-\ 2\,7\,5 \\
\hline
1\,2\,5
\end{array}
$$
<u>*2 subtracted from 3 = 1*</u> **answer**

Note: Once we found a neighbor to borrow from remember that it will be necessary to **go back** one place value at a time.

Subtraction

Addition to check subtraction

Remember to use addition, the opposite of subtraction, to check the answer of a subtraction problem.

EXAMPLE:

Check

we now add 21 and 52

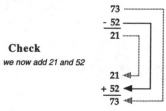

EXAMPLE:

Check

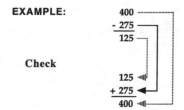

This is an excellent way to reinforce addition skills at the same time prepare students to use more than one operation in a math problem.

EXAMPLE: $4 + 2 - (3 + 1) =$ and so on....

Multiplication

How to Multiply

The opposite of division and it is also a faster way of adding. For example, here are 4 groups with 3 in each group. Show examples as often as possible and label whenever possible!

We can write a multiplication problem. Four groups with three in each group. *First*, we can write this as an addition problem:

$$3 + 3 + 3 + 3 = 12$$

Now as multiplication problem:

$$3 \times 4 = 12 \leftarrow \text{\textit{total from all groups}}$$

number in each group — *number of groups*

Product

When numbers are multiplied together the answer is called the product.

EXAMPLE:

$$2 \times 5 = 10$$

10 is the product of 2 x 5

Multiplication

Equality

As you might guess, *equality* is when items are equal in value. This can apply to money, time, weight, as well as numbers.

EXAMPLE: $\dfrac{1}{2} = \dfrac{2}{4} = \dfrac{3}{6}$

All have the same value.

Multiples

A given set of numbers another number can go into evenly.

EXAMPLE:

Let's take the number 3, it has the following multiples:

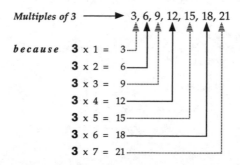

Multiples of 3 ⟶ 3, 6, 9, 12, 15, 18, 21

because

$3 \times 1 = 3$

$3 \times 2 = 6$

$3 \times 3 = 9$

$3 \times 4 = 12$

$3 \times 5 = 15$

$3 \times 6 = 18$

$3 \times 7 = 21$

Multiplication

Factors

Are those numbers multiplied together to get an answer (product).

EXAMPLE: $\mathbf{2} \times \mathbf{5} = 10$

The factors of **10** are 2 & 5 because 10 is the *product* of these two numbers multiplied together.

EXAMPLE: The factors of 24 are:

$$1 \times 24 = 24$$
$$2 \times 12 = 24$$
$$3 \times 8 = 24$$
$$4 \times 6 = 24$$

These are all the possible multiplication sentences that equal 24. So we can say that the numbers 1, 2, 3, 4, 6, 8, 12, and 24 are all factors of the number 24.

Prime Factorization

When we use only prime numbers to find a particular product.

EXAMPLE: The prime factorization for 24 is:

$$3 \times 2 \times 2 \times 2 = 24$$

➤ *Written as an exponent:* $3 \times 2^3 = 24$

2 and 3 are the prime factors of 24.
A factor tree can help you find prime factors!

Multiplication

Factor Tree

A factor tree is a way to find all the factors of a composite number. Using the number 10 (composite number) to show a factor tree, a student will be able to factor until there are only <u>prime numbers</u> left at the bottom of the tree.

EXAMPLES:

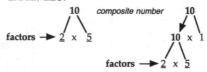

These are all the factors of 10 (1 & 10; 2 & 5)! Lets try a more complicated composite number. Notice the numbers at the bottom of the trees are prime. This will always be the case if we factor out all the numbers!

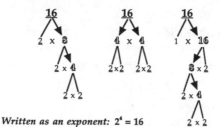

Written as an exponent: $2^4 = 16$

All numbers are factors of 16 (1, 2, 4, 8, 16). Again, all the bottom numbers (2) on the factor trees are **prime numbers**!

Multiplication

Inequalities

When 2 numbers do not have the same value. This can be written in the following ways.

EXAMPLE:

$$3 < 4 \quad or \quad 4 > 3 \quad or \quad 4 \neq 3$$

Definition of signs: < means less than; > means greater than; ≠ means not equal to (For the purposes of this book, this just means that 4 is not the same as 3.)

Multiplying by 10 , 100, 1,000

Is the same as moving the decimal point to the right or adding zeros to a given number.

EXAMPLE:

$$360 \times 1\underline{0} = 3,60\underline{0}$$

360 *becomes* 3,600

When there are no numbers to the right of the decimal point just add a zero (s) to satisfy the problem. When multiplying by 100 move the decimal point two places to the right.

$$360 \times 1\underline{00} = 36,0\underline{00}$$

Look at it this way, just add the zeros from one number to the end of the other number. Because:

$$360 \times 1 = 360 \quad and \quad 360 \times 1\underline{0} = 3,60\underline{0}$$

so

$$360 \times 1\underline{00} = 36,0\underline{00}$$

Multiplication

Multiplying positive and negative integers

When multiplying positive and negative integers we need to follow the chart below.

When multiplying:

A positive times a positive *the answer is* ***positive***.

$$+4 \times +4 = +16$$

A positive times a negative *the answer is* ***negative***.

$$+4 \times -4 = -16$$

A negative times a negative *the answer is* ***positive***.

$$-4 \times -4 = +16$$

Just multiply as you would any other numbers and remember the rules above. *See dividing integers for more instruction.*

Division

Definitions

The opposite of multiplication and a faster way to subtract. Division is when we have a large group of items that we break up into smaller equal groups. We can present this concept to our children using marbles, pennies, baseball cards, candy, etc. Have the items in one pile (group) and then do the *"one for me, one for you"* routine. This is division at its simplest form and kids can understand this concept because they have been doing it for years.

It is also important that we know a division problem when we see one.

EXAMPLE:

All the following are division problems.

$$48 \div 6 \quad \text{division}$$

$$\frac{48}{6} \quad \text{fraction}$$

$$6\overline{)48} \quad \text{division}$$

$$48:6 \quad \text{ratio}$$

All have an answer of 8. Even in the case of a *ratio* we must divide and in this case it would be 8:1 (8 to 1).

Because:

$$48:6 = \frac{48}{6} = 48 \div 6 = 6\overline{)48}$$

Division

Division Definitions

Dividend

Is the number that is divided by the divisor.

$360 \div 10 = 36.0$ where 360 is the dividend.

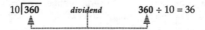

Divisor

The number that is divided into the dividend.

$360 \div 10 = 36.0$ where 10 is the divisor.

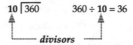

Quotient

When numbers are divided the answer is called the quotient.

$360 \div 10 = 36.0$ where 36.0 is the quotient.

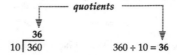

Division

How to divide

Continually follow the four step rule and you will never go wrong! Divide, multiply, subtract, and bring down.

EXAMPLE:

Divide 4 into 29

$$\begin{array}{r} 7 \\ 4\overline{)293} \end{array}$$

4 will not go into 2 so we move over one digit to 29 and 4 goes into 29 a total of 7 times

Multiply 7 x 4

$$\begin{array}{r} 7 \\ 4\overline{)293} \\ 28 \end{array}$$

7 x 4 = 28

Subtract 29 - 28

$$\begin{array}{r} 7 \\ 4\overline{)293} \\ -28 \\ \hline 1 \end{array}$$

29 - 28 = 1

Bring down the 3

$$\begin{array}{r} 73 \\ 4\overline{)293} \\ -28\downarrow \\ \hline 13 \\ -12 \end{array}$$

divide 4 into 13 three times

Do it all again

$$\begin{array}{r} 73\ r\,1 \\ 4\overline{)293} \\ -28 \\ \hline 13 \\ -12 \\ \hline 1 \end{array}$$

4 will not go into 1 so we have a remainder of 1

Division

EXAMPLE: With no remainder:

$$5\overline{)\begin{array}{r}6\\30\\-30\\\hline 0\end{array}}$$

Using the same 4 step rule divide, multiply, subtract, and bring down *if necessary*.

Dividing by 10, 100, 1000

Is the same as moving the decimal point to the left.

EXAMPLE:

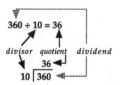

$$360 \div 10 = 36$$

divisor quotient dividend

$$10\overline{)360}$$

The decimal point is moved from 360. to 36.0 when dividing by 10. For every zero in the divisor move the decimal point one place to the left.

EXAMPLES:
$$360. \div 1\,\underline{0}\,\underline{0} = 3.60 \quad \text{move decimal left } \underline{2} \text{ places}$$
$$360. \div 1,\underline{0}\,\underline{0}\,\underline{0} = .360 \quad \text{move decimal left } \underline{3} \text{ places}$$
$$360. \div 10,\underline{0}\,\underline{0}\,\underline{0} = .0360 \quad \text{move decimal left } \underline{4} \text{ places}$$

Hint: As the decimal point moves to the left zeros must be placed to the left of the 3 in order to make the number correct.

Division

Multiplication to check division

Multiply the divisor by the quotient to find the dividend.

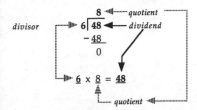

This division problem must have the correct answer because we multiplied the divisor by the quotient to find the dividend. Students often confuse the definitions for divisor, dividend, and quotient.

Dividing with different remainders

All this means is that we have some left over. We can write this as a decimal, fraction, or as a remainder. *Now try 27 ÷ 6 =*

EXAMPLE: *Remainder as decimal number:*

```
        4.5
    6 | 27.0      Add a zero & decimal point
      -24         to the dividend & quotient!
        30
      -30
         0
```

94

Division

EXAMPLE: *Remainder as a fraction:*

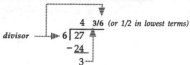

$$divisor \longrightarrow 6\overline{)27} \quad 4 \; 3/6 \;\; (\text{or } 1/2 \text{ in lowest terms})$$

$$\begin{array}{r} -24 \\ \hline 3 \end{array}$$

remainder $\longrightarrow \dfrac{3}{6} = \dfrac{1}{2}$ *Since we can not take 6 from 3*
divisor   *we write it as a fraction*

EXAMPLE: *Remainder as a remainder:*

$$\begin{array}{r} 4 \; r\,3 \\ 6\overline{)27} \\ -24 \\ \hline 3 \end{array}$$

Since we cannot take 6 from 3 we say that there is 3 left over or a remainder of 3. The letter **r** stands for remainder.

Division

Dividing with negative integers

At times our learners forget how to multiply, divide, add, or subtract negative integers. Remember, dividing negatives is the same as multiplying negatives for a positive or negative answer.

EXAMPLES:

Dividing *one negative* number your answer will be:

negative $^-4 \div {^+2} = {^-2}$

Dividing *two negative* numbers your answer will be:

positive $^-4 \div {^-2} = {^+2}$

Dividing with *all positive* numbers will always give you a:

positive $^+4 \div {^+2} = {^+2}$

Dividing an *odd* number of negatives will give you a:

negative $(^-12 \div {^-6}) \div ({^-4} \div {^+2}) = {^-1}$

Dividing an *even* number of negatives will give you a:

positive $(^-4 \div {^-2}) \div ({^-4} \div {^-2}) = {^+1}$

Division

Multiplying with negative numbers

Now we will check to see if multiplying the same numbers will give us a positive or negative answer. Remember, multiplying negatives is the same as dividing negatives for a positive or negative answer.

EXAMPLES:

Multiplying *one negative* number your answer will be:

negative   ⁻4 x +2 = ⁻**8**

Multiplying *two negative* numbers your answer will be:

positive   ⁻4 x ⁻2 = +**8**

Multiplying with *all positive* numbers will always give you a:

positive   +4 x +2 = +**8**

Multiplying an *odd* number of negatives will give you a:

negative   (⁻12 x ⁻6) x (⁻4 x +2) = ⁻**576**

Multiplying an *even* number of negatives will give you a:

positive   (⁻4 x ⁻2) x (⁻4 x ⁻2) = +**64**

Fractions

Definitions

A fraction is generally know as a part of a whole such as a dime is part of a dollar or *1/10 of a dollar*. Money is a good item to use to introduce the concept of fractions. Another good way to introduce fractions is to take a piece of paper and cut it in halves or fourths. Give one piece to your child and keep the other. Explain that they have 1/2 and you have 1/2. Now write the fraction 1/2 on each piece of paper.

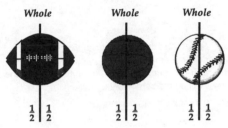

Whole	*Whole*	*Whole*
$\frac{1}{2}$　$\frac{1}{2}$	$\frac{1}{2}$　$\frac{1}{2}$	$\frac{1}{2}$　$\frac{1}{2}$

Denominator

The bottom number in a fraction.

EXAMPLE: In the fraction:

$$\frac{3}{4} \text{ ◁───── } denominator$$

The 4 is the denominator and the 3 is the numerator. This fraction means that we have 3 out of the 4 pieces left. Explain that the denominator is number of pieces we started with before any pieces were taken away.

Fractions

Numerator

The top number of a fraction.

EXAMPLE: In the fraction

$$\frac{3}{4} \text{———— numerator}$$

The 3 is the numerator and the 4 is the denominator. This means that we have 3 out of the 4 original pieces left.

Adding Fractions *(with the same denominator)*

If the denominators <u>are the same</u> simply add the numerators together. The denominator in the answer will be the same as the problem.

EXAMPLE:

$$\frac{3}{7} + \frac{2}{7} = \frac{}{7} \text{ place first}$$

Now add the numerators:

$$\frac{3}{7} + \frac{2}{7} = \frac{5}{7}$$

EXAMPLE:

$$\frac{4}{8} + \frac{3}{8} = \frac{}{8} \text{ place first}$$

Now add the numerators:

$$\frac{4}{8} + \frac{3}{8} = \frac{7}{8}$$

Fractions

Adding Fractions (with different denominators)

When we add fractions with *different denominators*
work to make the denominators the same. Here is
what we do!

To add the fractions:
$$\frac{2}{4} + \frac{3}{8} =$$

Our first step would be to change one denominator so that it is
the *same as the other*. In this problem it is easy to see that the
denominator of 4 can be changed to 8 simply by multiplying by 2.
What we do to the numerator we must do to the denominator!

Multiply x 2 $\quad \dfrac{2 \times 2}{4 \times 2} = \dfrac{4}{8}$

The denominators are now the same (8) and can be
added together:

now add $\quad \dfrac{4}{8} + \dfrac{3}{8} = \dfrac{7}{8}$

Remember, once the denominators are the **same** it is just a
matter of adding the numerators!!!

EXAMPLE:

$$\frac{1}{3} + \frac{3}{6} =$$

Convert 1/3 to a fraction with a denominator of 6.

$\dfrac{1 \times 2}{3 \times 2} = \dfrac{2}{6}$

now add $\quad \dfrac{2}{6} + \dfrac{3}{6} = \dfrac{5}{6}$

Fractions

Difficult Example: In column form

The lowest number (LCM) that 4 & 5 can go into is 20.

$$\frac{2}{5} \quad \text{needs to be changed to} \quad \frac{2 \times 4}{5 \times 4} = \frac{8}{20}$$

$$+\frac{1}{4} \quad \text{needs to be changed to} \quad +\frac{1 \times 5}{4 \times 5} = \frac{5}{20} \quad \text{denominators} \atop \text{are the same!!}$$

$$\frac{13}{20}$$

Just add the numerators $8 + 5 = \bigcirc$

Complete the problem:

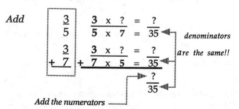

Add

$$\frac{3}{5} \quad \frac{3 \times ?}{5 \times 7} = \frac{?}{35} \quad \text{denominators}$$

$$+\frac{3}{7} \quad +\frac{3 \times ?}{7 \times 5} = \frac{?}{35} \quad \text{are the same!!}$$

$$\frac{?}{35}$$

Add the numerators

Subtracting Fractions (with the same denominator)

Similar to adding fractions because when we have the same denominators simply subtract the numerators.

EXAMPLE:

$$\frac{4}{8} - \frac{3}{8} = \frac{1}{8}$$

Fractions

Subtracting Fractions (with different denominators)

Remember, if the denominators are the same just add or subtract the numerator. If the denominators are different, multiply **one** denominator by a number to get the same denominator. Just like we did when we added fractions with different denominators.

Change the denominator

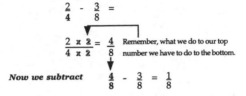

$$\frac{2}{4} - \frac{3}{8} =$$

$$\frac{2 \times 2}{4 \times 2} = \frac{4}{8}$$ Remember, what we do to our top number we have to do to the bottom.

Now we subtract $$\frac{4}{8} - \frac{3}{8} = \frac{1}{8}$$

Now what happens if both denominators require changing? The easiest way is to multiply each fraction by the other fractions denominator.

The fraction 3/4 and 5/7 cannot be added or subtracted in their present form so here is what we do. Multiply each fraction by the others denominator. Remember, what we do to the denominator we must do to the numerator!

EXAMPLE: 3/4 - 5/7 =

Multiply numerator x 7 $$\frac{3 \times 7}{4 \times 7} = \frac{21}{28}$$ $$\frac{3}{4} = \frac{21}{28}$$
Multiply denominator x 7

102

Fractions

Do the same to the other fraction to get the same
denominator. $3/4 - 5/7$

Multiply numerator by 4 $\dfrac{5 \times 4}{7 \times 4} = \dfrac{20}{28}$ $\dfrac{5}{7} = \dfrac{20}{28}$
Multiply denominator by 4

now add $\dfrac{21}{28} + \dfrac{20}{28} = \dfrac{41}{28} = 1\ 13/28$

or subtract $\dfrac{21}{28} - \dfrac{20}{28} = \dfrac{1}{28}$

Complete the problem:

$\dfrac{3}{5}$ $\dfrac{3 \times\ ?}{5 \times\ 7} = \dfrac{?}{35}$

$-\dfrac{3}{7}$ $\dfrac{3 \times\ ?}{7 \times\ 5} = \dfrac{?}{35}$ *same denominators*

subtract numerators ····▶ $\dfrac{?}{35}$

Multiplying Fractions

Multiply the numerators and the denominators.

EXAMPLE:

$\dfrac{3}{4} \times \dfrac{5}{7} =$

$\dfrac{3}{4} \times \dfrac{5}{7} = \dfrac{(3 \times 5)}{(4 \times 7)} = \dfrac{15}{28}$

103

Fractions

Multiplying mixed numbers

First eliminate the whole numbers and express as an improper fraction.

EXAMPLE: $2\frac{2}{3} \times 1\frac{4}{5} =$

Multiply numerators $\frac{8}{3} \times \frac{9}{5} = \frac{72}{15}$
Multiply denominators

Dividing Fractions

Fractions can be divided two ways, cross multiplying or inverting. Both use the same process but it is easier for kids to understand inverting (turning upside down or reversing) the second fraction.

EXAMPLE:

Using the equation:
$$\frac{3}{4} \div \frac{5}{7} =$$

We *always* invert the second fraction and change the ÷ sign to **X** then multiply. Look at our problem now:

$$\frac{3}{4} \div \frac{5}{7} =$$

$$\frac{3}{4} \times \frac{7}{5} = \frac{21}{20}$$

Cross Multiplying (follow the arrows 3/4 ÷ 5/7 = 21/20)

$$\frac{3}{4} \div \frac{5}{7} \longrightarrow \frac{21}{20}$$

Fractions

Fractions to decimals

To find the decimal equivalent of a fraction divide the denominator into the numerator.

EXAMPLE:

$$3/4 = .75$$

Will look like this $4\overline{)3}$

Since 4 will not *go into* 3 we need to add a decimal point and zeros (as many zeros as necessary) to satisfy our division problem.

$$4\overline{)3.\underline{00}}$$

First place a decimal point in the quotient (answer).

$$4\overline{)3.00} \quad now \; divide \quad 4\overline{)3.00} \\ \quad\quad\quad\quad\quad\quad\quad\quad \underline{-2\,8} \\ \quad\quad\quad\quad\quad\quad\quad\quad\quad 20 \\ \quad\quad\quad\quad\quad\quad\quad\quad \underline{-20} \\ \quad\quad\quad\quad\quad\quad\quad\quad\quad\; 0$$

Divide until there is no longer a remainder (until there is zero in the answer).

Problem Area: The important thing to remember is to place the decimal point in the quotient (answer) before you start to divide. This will eliminate any problems on where to place the decimal after an answer is found.

Fractions

Equivalent fractions

When 2 or more fractions are equal in value regardless of the numerator and denominator.

EXAMPLE:

$$\frac{2}{4} = \frac{3}{6} = \frac{4}{8} \quad \textit{All are half of a whole!}$$

These fractions are all equal to each other so they are all *equivalent fractions*. Each fraction just has a different number of pieces.

Improper fractions

A fraction that has a bigger (or equal) numerator than the denominator.

EXAMPLE:

$$\frac{3}{3} \quad \textit{or} \quad \frac{4}{3}$$

They are both improper fractions because they are equal or greater than one.

Note: Sometimes it is necessary to have an improper fraction, especially when we convert mixed numbers to improper fractions to multiple, add, subtract, or divide.

$$1\,^1/_3 \ = \ {}^4/_3$$

Fractions

Fractions to percent

This is the same process as converting fractions to decimals with one additional step. Divide the denominator into the numerator to find the decimal equivalent then move the decimal point two places to the right.

EXAMPLE: $3/4 = .75 = 75\%$

We divide the denominator into the numerator. Since 4 will not *go into* 3 we need to add a decimal point and zeros to satisfy our division problem.

$$4\overline{)3.\underline{0}\,\underline{0}}$$

First, place a decimal point in the quotient (answer) then divide.

$$
\begin{array}{r}
.75 \\
4\overline{)3.00} \\
-\underline{28} \\
20 \\
-\underline{20} \\
0
\end{array}
$$

To get the percentage move the decimal point two places to the right, add a % sign and this decimal .75 becomes 75.0% (3/4 = .75 = 75.0%).

$$.75 = 75.0\ \%$$

Look at these as **equal** $3/4 = 4\overline{)3} = .75 = 75\%$

Fractions

Reducing fractions to lowest terms

Reducing a fraction means to make the existing numerator and denominator as small as possible while keeping the fraction equivalent.

Reduce to lowest terms $\dfrac{15}{24}$

1) Find all the factors of both numbers.

2) Find the largest common factor.

3) Divide the numerator and denominator by the largest common factor.

$$\underline{15} = 1, \mathbf{3}, 5, 15$$
$$24 = 1, 2, \mathbf{3}, 4, 6, 8, 12, 24$$

3 is the largest or *greatest common factor* (GCF) of both the numerator and denominator.

$$\frac{15 \div 3}{24 \div 3} = \frac{5}{8} \ \textbf{\textit{(lowest terms)}}$$

Follow these three easy step and it will always give you the lowest term of a fraction!

Lowest terms for the obvious fractions

1) First, *always* look at the numerator.

2) Will the numerator divide evenly into the denominator?

3) If it does then this is the **G**reatest **C**ommon **F**actor (GFC)!

$$\frac{3 \div 3}{9 \div 3} = \frac{1}{3} \qquad \frac{4 \div 4}{16 \div 4} = \frac{1}{4} \qquad \frac{6 \div 6}{24 \div 6} = \frac{1}{4}$$

Fractions

Unlike fractions (also see adding & subtracting fractions)
Are fractions that do not have the same denominator.

EXAMPLE: 3/4 is *unlike* 5/7 because of the different denominators. To add or subtract these fractions we need to make the denominators the same by multiplying each fraction by the other's denominator.

$$5/\underline{7}$$

$$\frac{3 \times 7}{4 \times 7} = 21$$
$$= 28$$

$$\frac{3}{4} = \frac{21}{28} \text{ (These fractions are equivalent!)}$$

Now do the same to the other fraction:

$$3/\underline{4}$$

$$\frac{5 \times 4}{7 \times 4} = \frac{20}{28}$$

$$\frac{5}{7} = \frac{20}{28} \text{ (These fractions are equivalent!)}$$

Now both fractions have the same denominator. It is now just a simple matter of adding or subtracting the numerators. Then, if necessary, we can reduce to lowest terms.

now add $\frac{21}{28} + \frac{20}{28} = \frac{41}{28}$

or subtract $\frac{21}{28} - \frac{20}{28} = \frac{1}{28}$

109

Fractions

Improper fractions to mixed number

An improper fraction has a larger numerator than the denominator (4/3). A mixed number is a number with a whole and a fraction (1 1/3).

To change an improper fraction to a mixed number divide the numerator by the denominator.

EXAMPLE:

$$5/3 = ?$$

improper fraction $5/3 = \begin{array}{r} 1 \text{ r } 2 \\ 3\overline{)5} \\ -3 \\ \hline 2 \text{ (remainder)} \end{array} = 1\,2/3$ (mixed number)

so $5/3 = 1\,2/3$

our denominator stays the same

remainder 2 $5/3 = 1\,2/3$

our remainder is the numerator

one whole $5/3 = 1\,2/3$

our whole number

110

Fractions

Mixed numbers to improper fractions

The opposite process of converting an improper fraction to a mixed number.

EXAMPLE: $2\,3/4 = ?$

Step One $2\,3/4 = \ /4$ *Place the same denominator in our answer.*

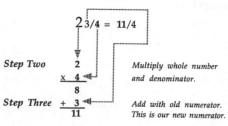

$$2\,3/4 = 11/4$$

Step Two

$$\begin{array}{r} 2 \\ \times\ 4 \\ \hline 8 \end{array}$$

Multiply whole number and denominator.

Step Three

$$\begin{array}{r} + 3 \\ \hline 11 \end{array}$$

Add with old numerator. This is our new numerator.

Step Four *Put it all together* $2\,3/4 = 11/4$

Another Way:

Denominator *times* whole number *plus* numerator!

Follow the arrows: $2\ 3/4 = \underline{11}$

$$4 \times 2 + 3 = 11$$

$$ 4$$

The denominator will stay the same!

111

Fractions

Subtracting fractions and whole numbers

This can be very confusing until we convert the whole number into a common fraction. Our learner must understand that we need to have a fraction in order to subtract another fraction.

EXAMPLE: $1 - 3/4 = ?$

Step One
Put in column form

$$\begin{array}{r} 1 \\ -\quad 3/4 \\ \hline \end{array}$$

Step Two

$$\begin{array}{r} 1 \\ -\quad 3/4 \\ \hline /4 \end{array}$$

We know our answer will have a 4 as the denominator because our problem has a 4 in the denominator.

Step Three
*Borrow from the whole number to make a fraction with the **same** denominator.*

$$\begin{array}{r} 0 \\ \cancel{1} = 4/4 \\ -\quad 3/4 \\ \hline /4 \end{array}$$

The 1 changes to 0 and makes a fraction of 4/4.

Now just subtract numerators then whole numbers, if necessary.

$$\begin{array}{r} 4/4 \\ -\ 3/4 \\ \hline 1/4 \end{array}$$

the **same** denominator

Fractions

Fraction Chart

1/2	= .50	= 50%	= $.50
1/3	= .33	= 33%	= $.33
1/4	= .25	= 25%	= $.25
1/5	= .20	= 20%	= $.20
1/6	= .165	= 16.5%	= $.17
1/7	= .142	= 14%	= $.14
1/8	= .125	= 12.5%	= $.13
1/9	= .111	= 11%	= $.11
1/10	= .10	= 10%	= $.10
1/11	= .0909	= 9%	= $.09
1/12	= .083	= 8.3%	= $.08
1/13	= .076	= 7.6%	= $.08
1/14	= .071	= 7.1%	= $.07
1/15	= .066	= 6.6%	= $.07
1/16	= .062	= 6.2%	= $.06
1/17	= .058	= 5.8%	= $.06
1/18	= .055	= 5.5%	= $.06
1/19	= .052	= 5.2%	= $.05
1/20	= .05	= 5%	= $.05

Decimals

Definitions

Decimals are like fractions because it is a way of expressing the concept of a *part of one*. As the numbers move to the right of the decimal point the place value becomes smaller.

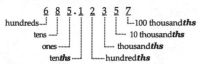

Problem Area

Our learners confuse whole number place value with decimal place value because of the similarity. Also, decimals are confusing because they start with the ten**ths** place value and not the ones place value. Teach your learner the meaning of the letters -th and that it means *part of* which also means it is on the right side of the decimal point.

Adding Decimals

Is no different then adding whole numbers. The trick is to keep each number in the proper place value (in straight columns).

EXAMPLE:

$$
\begin{array}{r}
1.89 \\
+2.47 \\
\end{array}
$$

··········· *place first*

$$
\begin{array}{r}
+1\ +1 \\
1.89 \\
+2.47 \\
\hline
4.36
\end{array}
$$
now just add

Hint: Make sure the decimal points of all the numbers being added are in line (underneath) with one another. Next, place the decimal point in your answer in line with the decimal points in your problem before adding the numbers.

Decimals

Subtracting Decimals (no borrowing)

Is the same as subtracting whole numbers. Always put the decimal point in the answer first, keep the decimal points in line, and do one column at a time.

EXAMPLE:

$$
\begin{array}{r}
2.47 \\
-\,1.32 \\
\hline
\end{array}
$$

place first

$$
\begin{array}{r}
2.47 \\
-\,1.32 \\
\hline
1.15
\end{array}
$$

now subtract

The same problem can be shown to our learners subtracting one column at a time:

from right to left

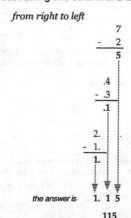

$$
\begin{array}{r}
7 \\
-\,2 \\
\hline
5
\end{array}
$$

$$
\begin{array}{r}
.4 \\
-\,.3 \\
\hline
.1
\end{array}
$$

$$
\begin{array}{r}
2. \\
-\,1. \\
\hline
1.
\end{array}
$$

the answer is **1 . 1 5**

Decimals

Subtracting Decimals (borrowing)

Same as borrowing when subtracting whole numbers. Place the decimal point in the answer before beginning to subtract.

EXAMPLE:

decimal points in line

$$
\begin{array}{r}
2.43 \\
-1.52 \\
\hline
\end{array}
\qquad
\begin{array}{r}
{}^{1}\ {}^{14} \\
\cancel{2}.\cancel{4}3 \\
-1.52 \\
\hline
.91
\end{array}
\qquad
\begin{array}{l}
\textit{The 4 borrows from the} \\
\textit{2, subtract one column} \\
\textit{at a time.}
\end{array}
$$

.   *place first*

Multiplying Decimals

This can be very confusing to our learners because of the decimal placement. Just remember how many decimal places we are multiplying together. If we multiply:

$$
\begin{array}{r}
.7 \\
\times\ .4 \\
\hline
.28
\end{array}
\qquad
\begin{array}{l}
\underline{\textbf{One}}\ \text{decimal place} \\
\underline{\textbf{One}}\ \text{decimal place} \\
\underline{\textbf{Two}}\ \text{decimal places}
\end{array}
$$

We can see there is one decimal place value in each number (.7 and .4) so our answer will contain two decimal places (.28).

A common mistake:

$$
\begin{array}{r}
.7 \\
\times\ .4 \\
\hline
2.8
\end{array}
\qquad
\begin{array}{l}
\text{One decimal place} \\
\text{One decimal place} \\
\textit{\textbf{Only one}}\ \text{decimal place}
\end{array}
$$

There should be two!

Decimals

Another common mistake:

This occurs when multiplying a whole number and a decimal number. Count the total number of decimal places in the problem and put the decimal point in the product (answer).

$$\begin{array}{r} 7 \\ \times\ .4 \\ \hline 2.\underline{8} \end{array}$$

One decimal place here
Only one decimal place here

Hint: Line up the digits, not the decimal points! This is different from what we learned when adding and subtracting other numbers. Lining up digits is easier than lining up by decimals.

EXAMPLE: (difficult)

$$\begin{array}{r} 28. \\ \times\ .35 \\ \hline \end{array}$$

It's much easier this way:

$$\begin{array}{r} 28 \\ \times\ .35 \\ \hline \end{array}$$

Count the number of decimal places in the problem and that's how many you have in the answer!

117

Decimals

Dividing Decimals

The easiest way to divide two decimal numbers is to change the divisor into a whole number.

EXAMPLE: $.4\overline{)\,.52}$

Change the .4 to a 4 by moving the decimal point one place to the right. We have to do the same thing to .52. Now we have this as our division problem:

$$4\overline{)\,5.2}$$

Next put a decimal point in the quotient (answer) and then divide. Remember, always line up the decimal points!

$$
\begin{array}{r}
1.3 \\
4\overline{)\,5.2} \\
-4 \\
\hline
1\,2 \\
-1\,2 \\
\hline
0
\end{array}
$$

More Examples:

$$.04\overline{)\,5.23} = 4.\overline{)\,523.}$$
$$.004\overline{)\,5.230} = 4.\overline{)\,5230.}$$

Note: Multiplying the numerator and denominator by 10 is the same thing as moving the decimal over <u>one</u> place to the right. This will change .4 to 4 and .52 to 5.2. When we multiply by 10 we move the decimal place one to the right in both the divisor and dividend.

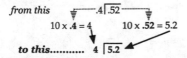

from this $.4\overline{)\,.52}$

$10 \times .4 = 4$ $10 \times .52 = 5.2$

to this........... $4\overline{)\,5.2}$

Decimals

Decimals to fractions

This depends on the value of the decimal number.

EXAMPLE:

$$.75 = \frac{75}{100}$$

First look at how many decimal places the decimal number uses. The number .75 uses two decimal places. So this decimal can be expressed as 75 hundredths or 75/100.

We can reduce this fraction to 3/4 (lowest terms) by dividing 25 from both the numerator and denominator. The largest number we can divide from the numerator and denominator is 25. *See Reducing Fractions*

$$\frac{75 \div \mathbf{25}}{100 \div \mathbf{25}} = \frac{3}{4}$$

Notice

$$.2 = \frac{2}{10}$$

$$.12 = \frac{12}{100}$$

Decimals to Percent

Just move the decimal point two places to the right.

EXAMPLE: .75 = 75%

If we are converting .75 to a percentage all we need to do is move the decimal point two places to the right.

$$.75 = 75.\%$$

More Examples:

.751 = 75.1%

1.75 = 175%

119

Geometry

Angles

Right Angle
An angle formed at the intersection of two perpendicular lines. A right angle measures of 90 degrees.

Acute Angle
An angle that measures from 0 degrees to less than 90 degrees.

Complimentary Angle
Are two angles that when added together form a 90º angle (right angle).

angle 1 = 30º

angle 2 = 60º   so 60º + 30º = 90º

Corresponding Angles
When a transversal line intersects two parallel lines there are angles formed that are equal. These are called *Corresponding Angles.*

transversal line ·········▮▮▮▶

angle 1 = angle 3 = angle 5 = angle 7
angle 2 = angle 4 = angle 6 = angle 8

if angle 1 = 60º angles 3, 5, and 7 are also 60º
if angle 2 = 120º angles 4, 6, and 8 are also 120º

Geometry

Angles continued

Obtuse Angle
An angle that measures greater than 90 degrees and less than 180 degrees.

Reflex Angles
Are angles that measure more than 180º and less than 360º.

Supplementary Angle
Are two angles when added together for a 180º angle (straight line).

Arc

Is the curve in any part of a circle. To find this *arc* we can use this formula:

$$(D/360) \times 2\pi r$$

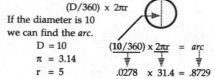

If the diameter is 10
we can find the *arc*.

$D = 10$
$\pi = 3.14$
$r = 5$

$(\underline{10}/360) \times 2\pi r = arc$

$.0278 \times 31.4 \approx .8729$

Area (see shapes)

Concave

Part of a shape that is curved inward.

concave side

121

Geometry

Congruence

When two items are exactly the same size and shape. Volleyballs can be considered congruent.

Convex

The part of a shape that curves outward.

convex side ·····⫸ **C**

Cosine

Is the ratio of the length of the side adjacent to an acute angle of a right triangle to the length of the hypotenuse.

$$cosine = \frac{adjacent\ side}{hypotenuse}$$

Diagonals

Are lines that connect vertices (corners) of a polygon.

All the thin lines are diagonals!

Line

Collection of solid dots that extends forever in both directions.

Geometry

Line Segment
Part of a line that has a beginning point and an end point. <u>Line Segment</u>

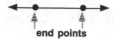

end points

Lines of Symmetry
A line that divides a figure into mirror images (exactly in half).

Parallel Lines
Lines that are equal distance apart at all points along each line.

Perimeter
The distance around (outer area) a closed figure such as a square, rectangle, or triangle.

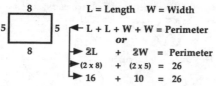

$L = Length \quad W = Width$

$L + L + W + W = Perimeter$
or
$2L + 2W = Perimeter$
$(2 \times 8) + (2 \times 5) = 26$
$16 + 10 = 26$

Ray
Part of a line that begins at a point (called an origin) and extends forever in the opposite direction.

origin

Geometry

Surface area

The amount of units necessary to cover the surface of a figure. Units can be in inches, feet, yards, etc.

Formula = **L x W** for a square or rectangle

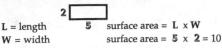

L = length   5   surface area = **L x W**

W = width   surface area = **5** x **2** = 10

Shapes

Square

A four sided shape where all the sides have equal length and four 90º angles.

area = **L x W**

area = 4 x 4 = 16

Triangle

A polygon with three angles and three sides.

area = 1/2 base x height **or base x height ÷ 2** (same thing)

height   *base*

base = 4   height = 3

$$\frac{(4 \times 3)}{2} = 6 \text{ (area)} \quad \textbf{or} \quad \textbf{\textit{(4 x 3) ÷ 2 = 6}}$$

Quadrilateral

Any four sided polygon.

Geometry

Circle

A round object that has the same radius and circumference in all directions.

radius ———◖▥┄┄┄*diameter*

circumference = $2\pi r$ or πd area = πr^2

$\pi = 3.14$ **r** = radius   **d** = diameter   **c** = circumference

The **radius** of a circle is half way across the circle from the center.

The **diameter** of a circle is the entire width of the circle through the center.

The **circumference** is the distance around the circle.

Polygon

Any multi-sided figure that is enclosed.   All squares, quadrilaterals, triangles, and hexagons are polygons.

Polyhedron

A solid shape (three dimensional).   Cubes, prisms, and pyramids are all examples of a polyhedron.

Rectangle

A four sided shape that has 2 sets of equal length.

Rhombus

Is a quadrilateral that is slanted.

Geometry

Sine

To find the sine of a right triangle we divide the length of the opposite side by the hypotenuse.

$$sine = \frac{opposite}{hypotenuse}$$
formula

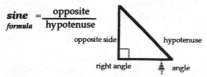

opposite side   hypotenuse

right angle   angle

Solids

Objects that have length, width, and depth (3 dimensions).

Tangent

The line that intersects (touches) the circle at only one point.

$$tangent = \frac{opposite\ side}{adjacent\ side}$$
formula

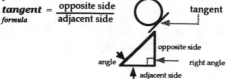

tangent

opposite side

angle   right angle

adjacent side

Triangles

Equilateral = All three sides & angles are equal to 60°.

Isosceles = Two sides are equal length.

Scalene = NO sides have equal length!

Right = Has one right angle (90°).

Obtuse = Has one obtuse angle (> 90° & < 180°).

Acute = Has one acute angle (less than 90°).

Geometry

Vertices

Are the corners (angles) within a polygon

The arrows point to the vertices.

Volume

The number of cubic units of a certain size that equals the space occupied by a geometric solid or *the amount of water a container will hold*. The cubic units can be any amount appropriate for measuring the volume in question. We can use gallons, wet yards, ounces, etc.

Volume Measuring

Cube Length x Height x Width *(depth)*

Pyramid $\dfrac{\text{Base x Height}}{3 \text{ (number of sides)}}$

Cylinder πr^2 x height

Cone $\dfrac{\pi r^2 \text{ x height}}{3}$

Sphere $\dfrac{4\pi r^3}{3}$

Algebra

In this section you will be able to see the basic fundamentals of the first year of algebra. Remember, this section is designed to give you a basic understanding of what can be a complex subject.

Algebra

Definitions

Algebraic Expression (or just called *expression*) are those math sentences that have variables and numbers in a logical order.

Associative Property states that it doesn't matter how you add a given group of numbers they will always equal the same value.

$5 + 10 + 13 = 28; \quad (5 + 10) + 13 = 28; \quad 5 + (10 + 13) = 28$

Binomials are those expressions that have ONLY two terms. $5x - 13$

Coefficient is a number that is multiplied by another number or variable. $3x$, where 3 is a coefficient of x.

Commutative Property states that no matter what order you place numbers in an addition or multiplication sentence the answer will always be the same. $2 + 3 = 5; \quad 3 + 2 = 5; \quad 2 * 3 = 6; \quad 3 * 2 = 6$

Complex Fraction are those fractions that have another fraction as a denominator or numerator.

$$\frac{\frac{1}{2}}{\frac{3}{4}} = 1/2 \div 3/4 = 1/2 \times 4/3 = 4/6 \text{ or } 2/3$$

Distributive Property says that we can multiply and add terms by distributing in a given way.
$3(2 + 6)$ is the same as $(3 * 2) + (3 * 6)$ both equal 24!

Algebra

Inverse Operation is a way to cancel another operation.

$$x * \frac{1}{3} = 9$$

To cancel out the 1/3 multiply each side by 3:

$$x * \frac{1}{3}(3) = 9 * 3 \quad x = 27$$

Like Terms are those terms that have the same letters raised to the same power. $3x$ & $2x$ are like term; $3x^2$ & $5x^2$ are like terms.

Monomials are those expressions that have only one term. $3x^2$

Polynomials are those expressions that have more than one term. $x^2 + 4x + 10$

Quadratic Equation is a polynomial equation which has a squared variable. $x^2 + 8x - 12$

Rational Expression is written as a fraction.

Radicals are those that have a "root" symbol. $\sqrt{}$

Radicand is the term inside the radical sign.
$\sqrt{9x^3}$ where $9x^3$ is the radicand

Standard Form in a polynomial equation is when all terms are in descending order according to their powers and variables. $x^2 + 4x + 10$

Trinomials are those expressions that have three terms. $x^2 + 4x + 10$

Algebra

Solving Linear Equations

Remember that you want to solve for the variable (unknown). First we have to isolate the variable on one side of the equal sign.

EXAMPLE:

$$3x - 10 = 26$$

Add 10 to both sides:

$$3x - \underline{\begin{matrix} 10 \\ +10 \end{matrix}} = \underline{\begin{matrix} 26 \\ +10 \end{matrix}}$$

Now we have: $3x = 36$

Divide the term by 3 get have the variable (x) all by itself:

$$\frac{3x}{3} = \frac{36}{3}$$

And the answer is: $x = 12$

Another Example: Fractions

$$\frac{2}{3}x = 4$$

Get rid of the fraction multiply each side by 3:

$$\frac{3}{1} * \frac{2}{3}x = 4(3)$$

$$2x = 12$$

Divide by 2

$$\frac{2x}{2} = \frac{12}{2}$$

$$x = 6$$

131

Algebra

Algebraic Fractions

First try to eliminate the fraction from at least one term in the equation.

EXAMPLE:

$$\frac{4x}{9} - \frac{1}{3} = \frac{x}{3}$$

Multiply each term by 9:

$$\frac{9}{1} * \frac{4x}{9} - \frac{1}{3} * \frac{9}{1} = \frac{x}{3} * \frac{9}{1}$$

We now have: $4x - 3 = 3x$

Isolate the variable by subtracting 3 from each side:

$$4x - \underset{+3}{\underline{3}} = \underset{+3}{\underline{3x}}$$

Now we have: $4x = 3x + 3$

Now subtract 3x from each side. This will isolate x on one side of the equal sign:

$$\underset{-3x}{\underline{4x}} = \underset{-3x}{\underline{3x}} + 3$$

Now we have: $x = 3$

Our answer is:

$$x = 3$$

Algebra

Polynomials & Monomials (add/subtract)

Very similar to adding or subtracting regular numbers but with one difference. We need to know what we can and cannot add or subtract.

We can only add or subtract like terms. This means it must have the same variables and the same exponents!

EXAMPLE:

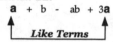

We only have two "like" terms so now we have:

$$4a + b - ab$$

EXAMPLE:

$$3x^2 + 7xy - 2x^2 + 7xy$$

Now combine like terms:

$$(3x^2 - 2x^2) + (7xy + 7xy)$$

$$x^2 + 14xy$$

As you can see in this equation it is just a matter of combining like terms and adding or subtracting the numbers (coefficients). The sign (**+** *or* **-**) in front of the term will determine what to do either add or subtract!

Algebra

Factoring GCF

Very similar to factor GCF in regular numbers. We have to find the largest number, variable, and exponent from all the terms.

EXAMPLE:
$$13a^4 + 39a^3$$

Step One: Factor the GCF from the number.
$$\mathbf{13}a^4 + \mathbf{39}a^3$$

13 is the largest factor of each number:
$$\mathbf{13}(a^4 + 3a^3)$$

Both terms have the variable "**a**" so we can factor out this variable to the smallest exponent value (a^3).
$$13(\mathbf{a}^4 + 3\mathbf{a}^3)$$

$$13a^3(a + 3)$$

Now Check:

$$13a^3 * a = 13a^4$$
$$13a^3 * 3 = 39a^3$$

$$13a^4 + 39a^3 = 13a^3(a + 3)$$

We must have it correct!

Algebra

Rules to Follow

Product Rule states that when we multiply exponents together it is the same as adding them.
$$a^2 * a^3 = a^{2+3}$$

Quotient Rule states that when we divide exponents it is the same as subtracting them.
$$a^3 = a^{3-2} \quad a^2$$

Other Rules:

$$(a^2)^3 = a^{2 \cdot 3}$$
if a = 3 $\quad (3^2)^3 = 3^6 = 729$

$$(ab)^3 = a^3 b^3$$
if a = 2 & b = 3 $\quad (2 * 3)^3 = 2^3 3^3 = 216$

$$(a/b)^3 = a^3/b^3$$
if a = 2 & b = 3 $\quad (2/3)^3 = 2^3/3^3 = 8/27$

$$a^{-3} = 1/a^3$$
if a = 2 $\quad 2^{-3} = 1/2^3 = 1/8$

Algebra

Solving Complex Fractions

Remember that a complex fraction is basically a fraction on top of another fraction. If we use the same rules for dividing regular fractions we will come up with the correct answer!

EXAMPLE: $\dfrac{\frac{1}{3}}{\frac{2}{3}}$ = 1/3 ÷ 2/3

We invert & multiple:

$$\frac{1}{3} \div \frac{2}{3} = \frac{1}{3} \times \frac{3}{2} = \frac{3}{6} = \frac{1}{2}$$

Now one with variables! $\dfrac{\frac{y-3}{y}}{\frac{y-3}{2y}}$ Follow the same rule!

Remove the middle division sign as follows:

$\dfrac{\frac{y-3}{y}}{\frac{y-3}{2y}}$ $\dfrac{y-3}{y} \div \dfrac{y-3}{2y} = \dfrac{y-3}{y} \times \dfrac{2y}{y-3}$

Invert and multiple:

$\dfrac{y-3}{y} \times \dfrac{2y}{y-3} = \dfrac{2y(y-3)}{y(y-3)}$ Note the like terms! They will cancel!

Now reduce algebraically by canceling like terms:

$$\frac{2\cancel{y}(\cancel{x-3})}{\cancel{y}(\cancel{y-3})} = \mathbf{2}$$

136

Algebra

Combining Like Terms

Adding all the variables (letters) that have the same power.

EXAMPLE:

In the expression

$$2x^2 + 2y^2 - x^2 + y^2$$

we combine the **x^2** and **y^2** terms

$$(2x^2 - x^2) \quad + \quad (2y^2 + y^2)$$

so now we have: $\qquad x^2 \qquad + \qquad 3y^2$

Multiplying Polynomials

The key is to multiply each term in one expression by all the terms in the other expression. Much like multiplying multi-digit numbers.

EXAMPLE: $(x + 2)(3x^2 + 2x - 5)$

Multiply the first **x** by all the other terms in the other expression: $(\mathbf{x} + 2)(3x^2 + 2x - 5)$

$x * 3x^2 = 3x^3$

$x * 2x = 2x^2 \qquad\qquad 3x^3 + 2x^2 - 5x$

$x * (-5) = -5x$

Now the 2: $(x + \mathbf{2})(3x^2 + 2x - 5)$

$2 * 3x^2 = 6x^2$

$2 * 2x = 4x \qquad\qquad 6x^2 + 4x - 10$

$2 * (-5) = -10$

Combine like terms: $3x^3 + (6x^2 + 2x^2) + (4x - 5x) - 10$

Now we have: $\quad 3x^3 \quad + \quad 8x^2 \quad - \quad x \quad - 10$

137

Algebra

Dividing Polynomials

The key is to separate each monomial.

EXAMPLE:

$$\frac{21x^2y - 12x^3y^3 - 9xy}{3xy}$$

Separate terms by monomial using the same denominator:

$$\frac{21x^2y}{3xy} - \frac{12x^3y^3}{3xy} - \frac{9xy}{3xy}$$

Now reduce to lowest terms. Keep in mind that when you divide variables it really means to subtract the exponents of each variable expression!

$$\frac{^7\cancel{21}x^2y}{3xy} \qquad 21 \div 3 = 7$$

$$\frac{7x^2y}{xy} \qquad x^2 - x = x \longrightarrow \mathbf{7x}$$

$$\qquad\qquad\qquad\qquad\qquad \textit{This is what's left!}$$

$$\frac{7xy}{y} \qquad y - y = 0$$

Again, do the same with the other monomials:

$$\frac{12x^3y^3}{3xy} \qquad 12 \div 3 = 4; \ x^3 - x = x^2; \ y^3 - y = y^2 \quad \mathbf{4x^2y^2}$$

$$\frac{9xy}{3xy} \qquad 9 \div 3 = 3; \ x - x = 0; \ y - y = 0 \qquad \mathbf{3}$$

Put it all together: $\mathbf{7x - 4x^2y^2 - 3}$

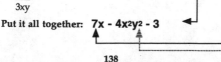

Algebra

Quadratic Equations

Solving for a variable in a polynomial equation is similar than solving for any variable. We must place all expressions to one side of the equal sign and zero on the other side of the equal sign. This is called *Standard Form*.

EXAMPLE: $x^2 + 2x - 15 = 0$

Notice that all terms are in descending order (largest to smallest) according to their exponents.

$$x^2 + 2x - 15 = 0$$

Next: Factor out the variable (x) for each expression.

$$x^2 + 2x - 15 = 0$$
$$(x - \textbf{?})(x + \textbf{?}) = 0$$

Next: This is the tricky part! Finding two numbers that when multiplied together equal -15 and when added together equal +2x. The first **?** will be 3 and the second **?** will be 5.

$$x^2 + 2x - 15 = 0$$
$$(x - \textbf{3})(x + \textbf{5}) = 0$$

$$x - 3 = 0 \text{ so } x = 3$$
$$\text{and } x + 5 = 0 \text{ so } x = -5$$

solution set $x = \{3, -5\}$

Algebra

Check: Now perform all the operations to check for accuracy.

$$(\mathbf{X} - 3)(\mathbf{X} + 5) = 0$$

$$\mathbf{X} * \mathbf{X} = \mathbf{x}^2$$

Next: Multiple each x by the digit in the other expression.

$$(\mathbf{X} - 3)(x + \mathbf{5}) = 0$$

$$\mathbf{X} * \mathbf{5} = 5x$$

Now the other x::

$$(x - \mathbf{3})(\mathbf{X} + 5) = 0$$

$$\mathbf{X} * \mathbf{-3} = -3x$$

Perform the operations:

$$5x$$
$$- 3x$$
$$\overline{2x}$$

Finally multiply the two digits together:

$$(x - \mathbf{3})(x + \mathbf{5}) = 0$$

$$\mathbf{-3} * \mathbf{5} = \mathbf{-15}$$

We must have factored correctly because all operations fit the equation.

$$x^2 + 2x - 15 = (x - 3)(x + 5)$$

Algebra

Quadratic Equations (that do not equal zero)

Remember to write the equation in standard form (0 on one side of =) before solving for the variable.

EXAMPLE: $x^2 + 8x + 15 = 3$

subtract 3 from each side

$$x^2 + 8x + \underline{\begin{array}{c} 15 = 3 \\ \textbf{-3} \quad \textbf{-3} \end{array}}$$

now we have standard form

$$x^2 + 8x + 12 = 0$$

Factor out the variable: $(\textbf{X} + ?)(\textbf{X} + ?) = 0$

Find two digits (numbers) that when multiplied together equal 12 and when added equal 8x:

How about 6 & 2: $(x + \textbf{6})(x + \textbf{2})$

Now we perform all operations to check:

$$x * x = \textbf{x}^2$$
$$6x + 2x = \textbf{8x}$$
$$6 * 2 = \textbf{12}$$
$$x^2 + 8x + 12 = 0$$

Sounds good to me! All are positive terms so we add all three together to check our answers. Our solution set (answer) is: $x = \{-6, -2\}$

Because $x + 6 = 0; \quad x = \textbf{-6}$
$x + 2 = 0; \quad x = \textbf{-2}$

Algebra

Solving Word Problems

The key is to give each unknown value the correct variable expression.

EXAMPLE:

If Bailey and Madison can kick a football a combined total of 100 yards but Joseph kicks the ball 10 yards farther than Bailey. How far can each one kick the ball?

Set the variable value:

$$X = \text{Bailey's kick}$$

$$X + 10 = \text{Madison's kick}$$

$$so \quad X + (X + 10) = 100 \text{ yards}$$

Now isolate the unknown value (X) on one side of the equal sign:

$$X + (X + 10) = 100$$

combine/add $\quad 2X + 10 = 100$

subtract $\quad \underline{-10 \quad -10}$

$$2X = 90$$

divide by 2 $\quad \dfrac{2X}{2} = \dfrac{90}{2}$

$$X = 45 \text{ yards (Bailey)} \quad so \quad X + 10 = 55 \text{ yards (Madison)}$$

Algebra

Rational Expressions
Add/Subtract

As with all fractions we must have the same denominator before adding or subtracting.

EXAMPLE:

$$\frac{24x}{6a} + \frac{12x}{3a} = ?$$

Multiply 3a by 2 to get 6a. Now we will have the same denominator.

$$\frac{24x}{6a} + \frac{12x * 2}{3a * 2} = ?$$

now add $\quad \dfrac{24x}{6a} + \dfrac{24x}{6a} = \dfrac{48x}{6a} = \dfrac{\cancel{6}(8x)}{\cancel{6}a} = \dfrac{8x}{a}$

EXAMPLE:

$$\frac{24x}{6} + \frac{12x}{3} = ?$$

$$\frac{24x}{6} + \frac{12x * 2}{3 * 2} = ?$$

$$\frac{24x}{6} + \frac{24x}{6} = \frac{48x}{6} = \frac{\cancel{6}(8x)}{\cancel{6}} = 8x$$

Algebra

Rational Expressions
Multiply/Divide

Remember how to multiply fractions? Same thing!
Multiply the numerators together and multiply the
denominators. Then we take one additional step by
canceling terms (reducing in effect).

$$\frac{9(x-3)^2}{7(y+8)} * \frac{7(y+8)}{3(x-3)}$$

Multiply numerators:

$$9(x-3)^2 * 7(y+8)$$

Multiply denominators:

$$7(y+8) * 3(x-3)$$

Put it all together:

$$\frac{9(x-3)^2 * 7(y+8)}{7(y+8) * 3(x-3)}$$

Now cancel terms: $(x-3)$ & $(y+8)$

$$\frac{9(x-3)^2 * 7(y+8)}{7(y+8) * 3(x-3)} = \frac{9(x-3) * 7}{7 * 3}$$

Now reduce: $9 \div 3$ & $7 \div 7$

$$\frac{^3 \, 9(x-3) * 7}{7 * 3} = 3(x-3) \textit{ is what is left}$$

Algebra

Radical Expression (simplified)

We must find a way to factor out a perfect square from underneath the radical sign.

EXAMPLE:

$\sqrt{72}$ does not have a perfect square

How about: $\sqrt{36 * 2} = \sqrt{72}$

Now we can take the square root of 36 out!

$\sqrt{72} = \sqrt{36 * 2} = \mathbf{6\sqrt{2}}$ (simplified)

In the following example you take the square root of an exponents is the same dividing by 2. The key is to find a number that we can easily factor out a square root! $\sqrt{x^8} = x^4$

EXAMPLE:

$\sqrt{28x^9y^6}$ Factor the number first!

$\sqrt{\underline{28}x^9y^6} = \sqrt{\underline{4} * \underline{7} * x^9y^6}$

Take out the square root of 4:

$\sqrt{\underline{4} * 7 * x^9y^6} = \underline{2}\sqrt{7 * x^9y^6}$

Factor the variables to make it possible to take out the square root:

$2\sqrt{7 * x^9y^6} = 2\sqrt{7 * \underline{x^8} * x * \underline{y^6}}$

Now we have: $2\sqrt{7 * \underline{x^8} * x * \underline{y^6}} = 2x^4y^3\sqrt{7x}$

Algebra

Radical Expressions (add/subtract)

You can only add/subtract radical expressions that have the same index (root) and radicand (expression under the radical sign).

EXAMPLE:

$$2\sqrt{75} - 2\sqrt{48}$$

We can simplify each expression like on the previous page.

$$2\sqrt{75} - 2\sqrt{48}$$

$$2\sqrt{25 * 3} - 2\sqrt{16 * 3}$$

Factor out the square roots of each expression:

$$2\sqrt{\mathbf{25} * 3} - 2\sqrt{\mathbf{16} * 3}$$

$$2 * \mathbf{5} * \sqrt{3} - 2 * \mathbf{4} * \sqrt{3}$$

$$10\sqrt{3} - 8\sqrt{3} = 2\sqrt{3}$$

Notice that in this example that each expression is a perfect square (25 = 5; 16 = 4) and the same radicand. Don't you wish they were all this easy!

Algebra

Radical Expression (multiplying)
We must multiply coefficients and radicands separately.

EXAMPLE:

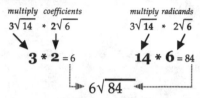

Now factor the radicand to find a perfect square:

$$6\sqrt{84} = \sqrt{4 * 21} \quad \text{(4 is a perfect square)}$$

Take out the square of 4 (which is 2):
$$6 * 2 * \sqrt{21}$$

Multiply: 6 by 2
$$12\sqrt{21}$$

This is our answer!

$$12\sqrt{21}$$

Algebra

Radical Expression (dividing)

Similar to other forms of division but with one extra step. We must remove the radical sign in the denominator before dividing.

EXAMPLE:

$$\frac{7}{\sqrt{5}}$$

Multiply both numerator & denominator by $\sqrt{5}$ to get rid of the radical sign.

$$\frac{7}{\sqrt{5}} * \frac{\sqrt{5}}{\sqrt{5}} = \frac{7\sqrt{5}}{5}$$

Rational Exponents

Just remember the numerator of a rational exponent is the power (exponent) and the denominator is the root.

EXAMPLE:

$$81^{1/2} = \sqrt{81} = 9$$

$$27^{2/3} = (27^{1/3})^2 = \left(\sqrt[3]{27}\right)^2$$

root ················· exponent

Algebra

Graphing

For the purposes of this book graphing is just a way of showing points (locations) much like we use longitude and latitude on a map. We use an "x" axis (up/down for east/west) and "y" axis (left/right for north/south). Our point of reference is where the two lines intersect (come together). At this intersection both axes have a value of zero.

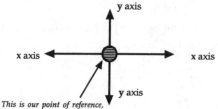

This is our point of reference,
x & y are both zero.

Notice the values for both x & y. The first quadrant both are positive. The second quadrant x is negative, y is positive. The third quadrant x is negative, y is negative. The fourth quadrant x is positive, y is negative.

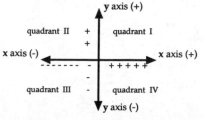

Algebra

Plotting

This means to find a spot on the graph of given coordinates. Remember that the first digit of each set is found on the "x" axis (**2**, 3) and the second digit is found on the "y" axis (2, **3**).

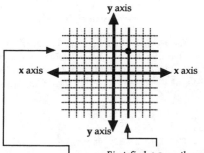

First find +2 on the x axis.
Now find +3 on the y axis.
Follow both lines until they intersect (meet).

Slope

Is defined as the ratio of rise (y axis) over run (x axis). This is just a matter of finding two points on the y axis and two points on the x axis. Once these points are found we can use our formula to find the slope.

$$\text{(slope) } m = \frac{y_2 - y_1}{x_2 - x_1}$$

If $y_2 = 4$ and $y_1 = 2$ $m = \frac{4-2}{8-3} = \frac{2}{5}$
If $x_2 = 8$ and $x_1 = 3$

Algebra

Graphing Linear Equations

Always remember that for any value given to x or y the statement must be true (in this case equal)!

EXAMPLE:

$$y = x + 3$$

If **x** is 2 than **y** must be 5 because: **$5 = 2 + 3$**

In this example we will give x three values. We will then solve for y. Next we will plot (find) each value and draw a line connecting each point on the graph. We will keep our equation:

$$\mathbf{y = x + 3.}$$

x Values: **Solve for y:**

x = 1	y = 1 + 3	y = 4
x = 2	y = 2 + 3	y = 5
x = 3	y = 3 + 3	y = 6

Next find each set of coordinates: (1, 4); (2, 5); (3, 6)

Remember, the first number is the x axis!

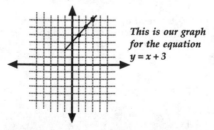

This is our graph for the equation $y = x + 3$

General Math Terms

In this section you will find terms used in many different areas of math.

General Math Terms

Absolute Value

The distance a number is from zero. For example, -7 and +7 have an absolute value of 7. Both -7 and +7 are 7 units away from zero. Written as |7| in a mathematical sentence.

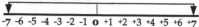

-7 -6 -5 -4 -3 -2 -1 **o** +1 +2 +3 +4 +5 +6 +7

Average

The sum (total) of a group of numbers added together then divided by the number of addends in that group. **Example:** The average of the numbers 25, 60, and 35 is found as follows:

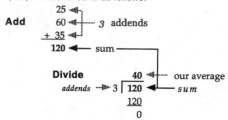

Add

    25
    60 ···· 3 addends
 + 35
  120 ◄— sum

Divide   40 ◄···· our average
addends ···► 3 ⌐120 ◄— *sum*
          120
            0

40 is the average

Another Example:

$$25 + 17 + 18 = 60$$

$60 \div 3 = 20$ *(our average)*

General Math Terms

Algebra

In simple terms it is the process of finding a value of an unknown quantity that uses variables.

> **EXAMPLE:**
>
> In the equation:
>
> $$3x + 2 = 8$$

We must find the value of the variable **x** (unknown) so that $3x + 2$ is equal to 8. Remember, in algebra, what we do to one side of the equal sign we have to do to the other! Here is how we isolate **x** on one side of the equal sign to find its value:

First, subtract **2** from each side of the equation because it will simplify the problem.

$$3x + 2 = 8 \qquad \underline{\text{From } 3x + 2 = 8 \text{ to}}$$
$$\underline{-2 \quad -2}$$

Now we have $3x = 6$ ◁┄┄┄┄┄┄┘

Divide each side of the equal sign by 3:

$$\frac{3x}{3} = \frac{6}{3}$$

The 3 in the numerator and denominator cancel each other out!

$$\frac{3x}{3} = \frac{6}{3}$$

$$x = \frac{6}{3} = 2$$

We have now solved the mystery of the value for x!

$$x = 2$$

154

General Math Terms

Capacity

The amount a container will hold.

EXAMPLE: quart, pint, cup, ounce, etc.

Composite Number

All whole numbers that have more factors than one and itself.

EXAMPLE: 4, 6, 8, 9, 10, 12, 14, 15

These are composite numbers because they have more than two factors.

Estimating

A faster way to find an answer when exact values are not needed. This is different from rounding because we round to the **largest** place value and **not** a **given** (specific) place value! Words like *about, around, almost, approximately* identify an estimation.

$$\begin{array}{r} \textbf{EXAMPLE:} \quad 426 \\ \textit{This is exact} \quad + \ 296 \\ \hline 722 \end{array}$$

↓

Now estimate **4**26   Find the highest place value.

\+ **2**96   We have at least 600!

↓

426   However, we must look at the next place

\+ 296   value to determine a true estimate.

426 is closer to.......... 400
and 296 is closer to... + 300
so our estimate is......... 700

155

Another   Example:

```
   1,250        1,000
  +2,789       +3,000
  ------       ------
   4,039        4,000
```

Expanded Notation

Naming the place value of each digit. For example, the number 122,685 is written in expanded notation this way:

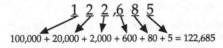

$$100,000 + 20,000 + 2,000 + 600 + 80 + 5 = 122,685$$

Exponents

Shows the number of times the base number is multiplied by itself and an easier way to express larger numbers.

EXAMPLE: $3 \times 3 \times 3 \times 3 = 3^4 = 81$

base number ⟶ 3^4 ⟵ exponent

so $3 \times 3 \times 3 \times 3 = 3^4 = $ 3 to the fourth power

Another way to look at it!

$$3 \times 3 = 9$$
$$9 \times 3 = 27$$
$$27 \times 3 = 81$$

Notice the 4 threes!

General Math Terms

Greater than; less than; not equal to

The *greater than* (>) sign is used to identify one number as the larger of two numbers. For example, the problem that 25 is *greater than* 10 can be written as follows: **25 > 10**

The *less than* (<) sign is used to identify one number as the smaller of two numbers. For example, 10 is *less than* 25 can be written as follows: **10 < 25**

The *not equal to* (≠) sign just means two numbers or equations are not equal: **2 + 5 ≠ 3 + 7**

Remember, the first number (left to right) is always our point of reference or starting point.

Integers (also see *Multiplying*)

All positive and negative whole numbers including zero.

EXAMPLE: -4, -3, -2, -1, 0, 1, 2, 3, 4 *are all integers.*

Adding & Subtracting

An easy way to remember how to add or subtract integers is to use a number line. Find the <u>first number</u> in the problem then follow the appropriate rule:

*When we **add** a **positive** we move to the **right** on the number line.*

EXAMPLE: 2 + 3 = ⁺5

Find ⁺2 on the line then <u>add</u> 3 (move right):

157

General Math Terms

Integers continued

When we **subtract** a **positive** we move to the **left** on the number line.

EXAMPLE: 5 - (+3) = +2

Find +5 on the line then <u>subtract</u> 3 (move left):

When we **add** a **negative** we move to the **left** on the number line.

EXAMPLE: 5 + (⁻3) = +2

Find +5 on the line then <u>subtract</u> 3 (move left):

When we **subtract** a **negative** we move to the **right** on the number line.

EXAMPLE: 2 - (⁻3) = +5

Find +2 on the line then <u>add</u> 3 (move right):

Always start with the first number (positive or negative) in the problem and find it on the number line. Then add or subtract (move left or right) on the number line.

General Math Terms

Least Common Multiple (LCM)

Is the lowest number that a group of numbers can divide into (without a remainder). For example, the lowest number (or LCM) that both 3 and 4 can go into is 12. Here is how we came to this conclusion:

Here are multiples of 3   3, 6, 9, **12**, 15, 18, 21, 24.....

Here are multiples of 4   4, 8, **12**, 16, 20, 24, 28......

The **LCM** for 3 and 4 is **12**.

Mixed Numbers

A number that contains both a whole number and a fraction.

EXAMPLE: $2\ 2/3$ is a mixed number.

whole number ⌐   └ fraction

Mean

The *average* of a given group of numbers. For example, the mean of the numbers 5, 4, 9, 2 is 5 because:

$$\underline{5} + \underline{4} + \underline{9} + \underline{2} = 20$$

$$20 \div 4 = 5$$

$$\begin{array}{r} 5 \leftarrow\text{Mean} \\ 4\,\overline{\smash{\big)}\,20} \end{array}$$

159

General Math Terms

Median

The middle number in a given set of numbers.

EXAMPLE:

In the set   1, 2, 3, 4, 5, 6, 7, 8, 9

The median or the middle number in the set is 5.

Measurements

| (standard) | (metric) |

The standard unit of measure:

for the UNITED STATES	THE REST OF THE WORLD
12 inches = 1 foot	1 meter = 10 decimeters
3 feet = 1 yard	1 meter = 100 centimeters
1760 yards = 1 mile	1 meter = 1,000 millimeters
5280 feet = 1 mile	1 kilometer = 1,000 meters
	1 kilometer = 10,000 decimeters
8 ounces = 1 cup	1 kilometer = 100,000 centimeters
2 cups = 1 pint	1 kilometer = 1,000,000 millimeters
2 pints = 1 quart	
4 quarts = 1 gallon	*As you can see this unit of measure is based on multiplying or dividing by 10, 100, or 1,000 much like our monitory system.*

Mode

Is the number or data that occurs most often.

In the numbers: 2, 3, **5**, 6, 9, 8 , **5**

The mode is **5** because it occurs most often.

General Math Terms

Money

A great way to introduce many aspects of math.

EXAMPLES:

\$.01 = 1/10 of a dime = 1/100 of a dollar
It takes 100 pennies to make a dollar

\$.05 = 1/2 of a dime = 1/20 of a dollar
It takes 20 nickels to make a dollar

\$.10 = 1/10 of a dollar   *It takes 10 dimes to make a dollar*

\$.25 = 1/4 of a dollar   *It takes 4 quarters to make a dollar*

If you'll notice the denominator is how many we need to make one whole.

100 pennies make a dollar	/100
20 nickels make a dollar	/20
10 dimes make a dollar	/10
4 quarters make a dollar	/4

Number Line

Helps in visualizing addition and subtraction problems.

$$^-4 \quad ^-3 \quad ^-2 \quad ^-1 \quad 0 \quad ^+1 \quad ^+2 \quad ^+3 \quad ^+4$$

Order of Operation

Here are the rules for doing problems with more than one math function. Do parentheses, exponents & roots, multiplication & division, addition & subtraction in that order!

1. Do parentheses $(3 + 4) \times 2^2 = 28$

2. Exponents and roots $2^2 \times 4 = 16$

3. Multiplication or Division (from left to right) $3 + 4 \times 2 = 11$

4. Addition or Subtraction (from left to right) $4 + 2 - 3 = 3$

161

General Math Terms

Place Value

In a number each digit has a different value. In the number 1,573:

        The digit 1 = 1,000
        The digit 5 =   500
        The digit 7 =   70
        The digit 3 =   3

Values   1 2 6, 9 4 7, 8 6 2, 0 9 6

- ones
- tens
- hundreds
- one thousand
- ten thousand
- hundred thousand
- one million
- ten million
- hundred million
- one billion
- ten billion
- hundred billion

Hint: In the number 2,222 each 2 has a different value. Because the <u>value</u> of a digit depends on the <u>place</u>. Use money as an example. Which digit holds the highest value in the number $202? The two in the hundreds place or the two in the ones place?

Powers of 10

Is a faster way to express very large numbers with 10 as the base number (see exponents). Notice that the exponent (4) also gives us the number of zeros in the final answer.

EXAMPLE: ⌐ exponent

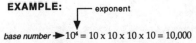

base number ➤ $10^4 = 10 \times 10 \times 10 \times 10 = 10,000$

162

General Math Terms

Prime Numbers

Are those numbers that have only two factors (1 and itself). For example, 5 is a prime number because the only way to get a product **(using only whole numbers in a multiplication problem)** of 5 is to multiple 1 x 5 = 5. As the definition states, a prime number only has two factors, 1 and itself. The number 4 has 1, 2, and 4 as factors so it is <u>not</u> a prime number, it is a composite number.

Prime Numbers:

2-3-5-7-11-13-17-19-23-29-31-37-41-43-47-53-59-61

Notice that all prime numbers are odd numbers with the exception of the number 2.

Prime Factorization

Is when you factor (take out) only prime numbers out of a given composite number (non prime). For example, 30 can be expressed in a math sentence as:

$$2 \times 15 = \mathbf{30} \longleftarrow \textit{composite number}$$

However, this is not prime factorization because 15 is not a prime number. To use prime factorization we must use <u>only</u> prime numbers as factors. What prime numbers can we use to factor out of 15? How about 3 & 5? Here is how we use prime factorization for the number 30.

$$2 \times \underline{15} = 30$$

Is now expressed: $2 \times (\mathbf{3 \times 5}) = 30$

Prime numbers are 2, 3, and 5. *<u>This is prime factorization</u>*.

General Math Terms

Probability

The likelihood that something will occur. This is written as:

PROBABILITY = $\dfrac{\text{number of favorable outcomes}}{\text{number of possible outcomes}}$

EXAMPLE:
If we roll a die once there is a one in six (1/6 or 1:6) chance that we will roll a 5. This is because there are six numbers on a die and only one is the number 5.

Proportions

Two equivalent ratios. Say two out of four children like pizza. This means that for every four children, two will like pizza. This can be reduced to lower terms and we could say for every two children one will like pizza.

EXAMPLE: Written as a fraction:

$$\frac{2}{4} = \frac{1}{2}$$

EXAMPLE: Written as a ratio:

$$2{:}4 = 1{:}2$$

For every four kids two will like pizza, for every two kids one will like pizza, and so on.

Pythagorean Theorem

In any right triangle with sides *a* and *b* and hypotenuse side *c*. For example:

$$a^2 + b^2 = c^2$$

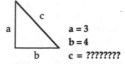

$a = 3$
$b = 4$
$c = ????????$

Using the formula $a^2 + b^2 = c^2$ we can find the answer.

$$a^2 + b^2 = c^2$$

$$3^2 + 4^2 = c^2$$

$$9 + 16 = c^2$$

$$25 = c^2$$

Now we know that c^2 is 25. What is c? Find the square root of 25 and you will have solved the value of c.

$$\sqrt{25} = \sqrt{c^2} = \sqrt{5^2}$$

the $\sqrt{5^2}$ is........ 5

General Math Terms

Range

From the lowest (fewest) to the highest (most) in a set of numbers.

EXAMPLE:

In the set of numbers:

$$5, 10, 25, 79, 81, 82$$

The range is **77** because counting from 5 to 82 equals 77.

We can just subtract the smallest number from the largest number: $82 - 5 = 77$

So, once again, the range is **77**.

Rational Numbers

Any positive or negative number. Numbers can be:

composites (2, 4, 6, 8)
primes (2, 3, 5, 7)
fractions (2/4)
improper fractions (4/3)
mixed numbers (3 3/4)
variables (x)
integers (⁻4 or +4), etc.

Ratios

Is a comparison of two numbers by division. For example, the ratio of 1 to 5 can be written as a fraction 1/5 or as a ratio 1:5. This means one out of every 5.

General Math Terms

Reciprocal

Two numbers that are multiplied together and their product is equal to 1.

EXAMPLE:

$$\frac{3}{4} \times \frac{4}{3} = \frac{12}{12} \text{ or } 1$$

3/4 and 4/3 are reciprocals

Another way of looking at reciprocals is just inverting the fraction (turning upside down).

Roman Numerals

Are numbers that are represented by letters. Although their usage has diminished over the years they are still used in outlining, older movies, and the Superbowl.

EXAMPLES:

$$I = 1 \quad V = 5 \quad X = 10 \quad L = 50$$
$$C = 100 \quad D = 500 \quad M = 1000$$

Here is the difficult aspect of this numbering system. How do we write numbers such as 4? When a smaller value symbol is before (left to right) a larger symbol we subtract the value of the smaller symbol.

EXAMPLE: IV = 4 (5-1)

I is smaller then V so we subtract one from five.

Others:

| IX = 9 (10-1) | CM = 900 (1,000-100) |
| IL = 49 (50-1) | IC = 99 (100-1) |

General Math Terms

Smaller symbols in front of larger symbols we add.

EXAMPLE:

VI = 6 (5+1)

XI = 11 (10+1)

LX = 60 (50+10)

MCX = 1,110 (1,000+100+10)

Rounding

Is similar to estimating because we round numbers to make it easier to calculate an answer. The key is to know what number we want to round. **EXAMPLE:** We want to round the number 1,573 to the nearest tens place value. Follow the rules to make it simpler.

Rules

1. Identify the digit (place value) we want to round: *tens*

   1,5$\overline{7}$3

   In this case we want to round to the tens place value.

2. Look at the digit immediately to the right of the 7, we find it is the digit 3 (1,57**3**).

3. If the 3 were **five** or larger, the 7 should change to an eight. However, if the digit is **four** or less the 7 should remain a 7. In this case the 7 will remain a 7.

4. After we round to the tens place we change all the smaller digits to zero (157**0**).

5. Now the number has changed from 1,573 to 1,570. We rounded to the nearest tens place value.

General Math Terms

Rounding continued

Round to the nearest 10,000 place value:

Identify place value:	1,5<u>6</u>7,543
Look at the number to the right:	1,56<u>7</u>,543
7 is larger than 4 so we round up to:	1,57
6 rounds to 7 and all the other	1,57<u>0,000</u>
smaller place values turn to zero:	

from 1,567,543 *to* 1,570,000

Hint: Tell your kids to identify the place value to be rounded and then the number to the right. Often times kids look at large numbers and they are overwhelmed. They only need to worry about two place values (two digits)!

Scale

Drawing items smaller than their original form but drawing everything with the same (fixed) proportions. This is used when drawing items larger than the paper being used, such as maps and buildings.

EXAMPLE:

This could be the scale drawing of a football field where every inch equals 3,600 inches or 1:3,600 scale.

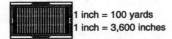

1 inch = 100 yards
1 inch = 3,600 inches

General Math Terms

Scientific Notation

A faster way to show mathematical expressions using exponents. For example, a normal multiplication sentence can look like this:

$$6 \times 1,000 = 6,000$$

Using scientific notation, the same math sentence looks like this:
Notice the exponent equals the number of zeros!

$$6 \times 10^3 = 6,000$$

The decimal point moves to the right when there is a positive exponent:

$$6.2195 \times 10^4 = 62,195.0$$

With positive exponents (10^4) the decimal point moves to the right **4** places to make the number larger. Now look at the same problem using a negative exponent:

$$62,195.0 \times 10^{-4} = 6 . 2 . 1 . 9 . 5 . 0$$

end here   4   3   2   1   **start here**

With a negative exponent the decimal point is moved to the left **4** places to make the number smaller. If there are no more digits on the left add zeros to make the number correct.

$$57 \times 10^{-4} = .0057$$

$$.0057.$$

to here   ◄——►   **from here**

Move to the left **4** decimal places making it smaller.

General Math Terms

Square

When a number is multiplied by itself the number is said to be squared. All of the following mean the same thing:

EXAMPLE:

$$4 \times 4 = 16$$
$$4^2 = 16$$

4 squared is 16

16 is the square of 4

and 4 is the square root of 16

Square Root

A square root is a product of a number multiplied by itself.

EXAMPLES:

$4 \times 4 = 4^2 = 16$	The square root of 16 is **4** ($\sqrt{16} = 4$)
$5 \times 5 = 5^2 = 25$	The square root of 25 is **5** ($\sqrt{25} = 5$)
$6 \times 6 = 6^2 = 36$	The square root of 36 is **6** ($\sqrt{36} = 6$)
$7 \times 7 = 7^2 = 49$	The square root of 49 is **7** ($\sqrt{49} = 7$)

Temperature Converting

	freezing	boiling
Fahrenheit	32°	212°
Centigrade	0	100

How to convert:

Fahrenheit to Centigrade:

$$\frac{5(F-32)}{9}$$

Centigrade to Fahrenheit:

$$\frac{(C \times 9)}{5} + 32$$

171

General Math Terms

Time

If your children are just learning to tell time it may be easier to start with a digital clock. You can use television listings to help them understand the concept of the hour and half hour. As they advance this would be a good way to introduce fractions such as 1/2 and 1/4.

1/2 past the hour

1/4 past the hour

Variables

A symbol that stands for a number. This symbol is usually a letter.

$3\underline{n} + 2 = 8$

Variable Expression

Is an expression that contains at least one variable.

EXAMPLE:

$3n + 2 = 8$

n is the variable in this equation

Weights (see Measurements)

General Math Terms

Greatest Common Factor (GCF)

The largest number that can be factored into any given set of numbers. For example, the numbers 10 & 15 have a GCF of 5 because 5 is the largest common factor of 10 & 15. This is a simple problem. However, most of the time it is necessary to find several factors in a given set of numbers before determining the *GCF*. For example, what is the *GCF* of 48 and 72? First, find all the factors of 48 & 72.

48 has the following factors:

$$1, 2, 3, 4, 6, 8, 12, 16, 24, 48$$

72 has the following factors:

$$1, 2, 3, 4, 6, 8, 9, 12, 18, 24, 36, 72$$

What is the largest factor (GCF) of both numbers? The answer is 24.

Another EXAMPLE:

44 has the following factors: 1, 2, 4, 11, 22, 44

40 has the following factors: 1, 2, 4, 5, 8, 10, 20, 40

What is the **GCF** of 44 and 40? The answer is 4.

General Math Terms

Solving Word Problems

Most learners have difficulty solving word problems because they **do not** know how to identify the important information. Just like every other part of this book we only look at one small portion of information or data at a time!

Here we go.....

1) Make a list of all numbers in the problem.

2) Identify what type of answer is required by viewing key words in the problem. *See key words below*

Key Words

Addition	Subtraction	Multiplication	Division
all together	difference	all groups	in each
in all	remain	product	separate
total	left	by	each group
together	less	times	split
sum	change	of	
both/all	fewer		

3) Cross out all unimportant information so not to confuse the learner.

4) Put all the important numbers in a mathematical expression.

EXAMPLE:

Dan and ***Mandy*** went to Six Flags for the 4th of July. At the end of the day they ***split*** the remaining *$12.50*. How much did Mandy have to spend for dinner on the trip home?

Key Words	Math Expression
2 *(people)*	$12.50 ÷ 2 =
split *(division)*	
$12.50	